STEVEN CANEY'S
PLAY
BOOK

STEVEN CANEY'S
PLAY
BOOK

WORKMAN PUBLISHING COMPANY
NEW YORK CITY

WP

Library of Congress Cataloging in Publication Data

Caney, Steven.
    Steven Caney's playbook.
    SUMMARY: Projects, constructions, games,
puzzles, and other activities for children organized
according to the spaces where they play.
    1. Handicraft—Juvenile literature.
    2. Games—Juvenile literature.
    [1. Handicraft. 2. Games]
I. Title. II. Title: Playbook.
TT160.C34   649'.51   75-9816
ISBN 0-911104-37-2
ISBN 0-911104-38-0 pbk.

Cover Design: Paul Hanson
Cover Photograph: Kathryn Abbe
Book Designer: Bernard Springsteel
Illustrations: Tom Cooke
Photographs: Steven Caney
Typeset: Innovative Graphics International Ltd.
Printed and Bound by the George Banta Company
Manufactured in the United States of America

Workman Publishing Company
231 East 51st Street
New York, New York 10022

First printing, June 1975

*To my parents
and the wonderful
play treasures
they kept
in the basement*

My warmest appreciation to my best friend and wife Shelly, who wisely offered suggestions and graciously accepted the grunt jobs, to our children Jennifer and Noah, who so enthusiastically inspire imagination and fun, to Tom Cooke, John Newman, and Reuben Klickstein, whose professional expertise made my efforts such a delight, and to all the kids who came to play with my toys: Gretchen, Murray and Susie Anderegg, David Bagnell, Billy and

Chriss Belanger, Zachary Bell, Mindy and John Berman, Cheryl Bernier, Jennifer and Noah Caney, Lee and Leslie Caney, Julia and Kate Carpenter, Todd Cooke, Mary, Barbie, and Patty Culkins, Alice Deacon, Billy and Brian Driscoll, Michael Evans, Bobby and Scottie Forsberg, Owen Freeman, Bobby Hooper, David, Daniel, and Jodie Hurwitz, Sarah Ingersoll, Jamie and Kim Klickstein, Mary LaBonte, Cindy Liessner, Sam Meade, Marta Miskolczy, Nelly (Dog), Michael and Peter Orszag, Ethan Owens.

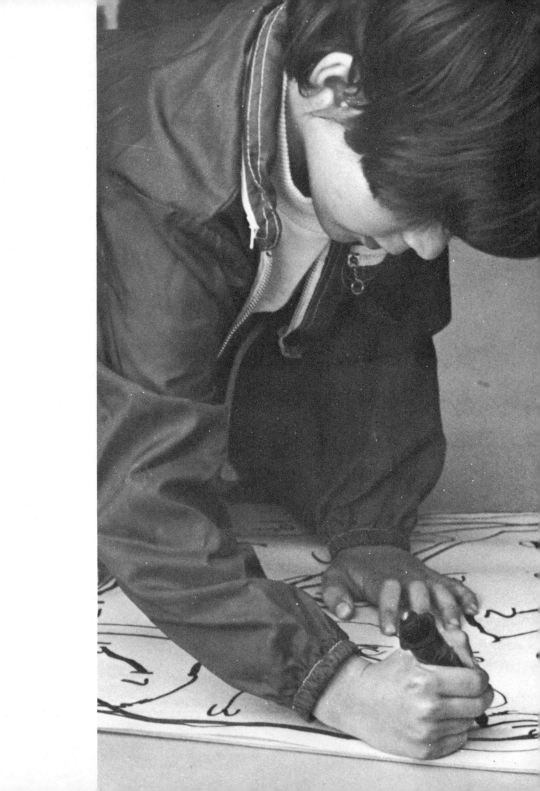

CONTENTS

FOREWORD TO PARENTS

Kids are incorrigible players. Wherever a child may be, he will consider it a space for play and find something there to play with. The kitchen with its cooking utensils and tempting ingredients becomes a laboratory for making strange concoctions, the workshop equipped with machinery or just a few hand tools invites the child to build the way parents do, and even the bathroom promises enticing water play or pretend "chemistry" experiments. Basements, beds, garages, closets, porches, steps, and yards need only a child's incentive and imagination to turn them into play spaces. Much of the time, however, a child's play area is confined to a few "acceptable" spaces. A kid is allowed to use his bedroom or playroom only, with its familiar stock of books, games, and bin of scrap materials. If given the freedom, a child would probably choose the entire house as his play area as well as those "adult" environments which usually intimidate him.

Play comes naturally to kids and it is difficult for them to be patient where they cannot play. Eating at a restaurant usually finds the kids "itchy" until the food is served, then wanting to leave and showing it by playing under the table. A day trip in the car can begin with anxious expectations, but when looking at the scenery becomes tedious, a child's uneasiness often leads to complaining that upsets everyone. Kids are often carted along to stores where everything that seems fun to do is forbidden. How can a child use his whole environment for play while satisfying his parents that the experience will be safe and sane for them both?

PLAYBOOK is the answer. It is everything to do and everywhere to do it for kids three years old, up to and including adults. The book contains more than seventy activities and projects to do, to make, and to play with wherever children are. They use only discards and inexpensive materials found around the house, or at places kids often visit—things like straws, paper cups, cardboard, old tires, pencil and paper, wood scraps, playing cards, and various art materials. PLAYBOOK shows how to make and play solitaire games, competitive games, quiet activities for indoors, active play projects for open spaces, pencil and paper games, work shop constructions, kitchen recipes, magic tricks, puzzles to solve, things to give, and toys that race, play music, and fly! While all are complete projects in themselves, each provides incentive, and stimulates the

13

imagination for further self-starting play.

Children's playthings haven't changed much during the last hundred years. Many of the games and toys children play with today are the same types of things their parents, grandparents, and great-grandparents played with when they were young. Some of the projects in PLAYBOOK come from those traditional sources, including folk toys, commercial toys, street games, and people who were willing to share their childhood favorites. Some of the activities are true inventions—games and toys that have never been made before. Though all the projects will, of course, be handmade, they are not "craftsy." The child does not have to be concerned that his construction is pretty. The idea is to put materials together to produce playthings that work and are fun. All the projects in PLAYBOOK have been easily constructed and played with by many children of different ages and abilities.

One of the nice discoveries made by kids (and parents) in using PLAYBOOK is that good toys do not have to be bought in stores. The toys and games which turn out to be really the most fun are those a child builds himself. A homemade toy has a personality that no store-bought toy can ever acquire. Children do not start a project because they feel they are doing something useful, or as a way to save money, but are attracted by the idea of messing around and having the freedom to invent and build something unique, something original that they can call their own. The finished product is quite impressive to the child because he put it together himself and it really works; moreover, if a homemade toy breaks, the child knows how it went together, so he can easily fix it. Children

who become comfortable with building from scraps and discards are not so quick to demand store-bought toys. The independence of "making your own" develops into an ability to create one's own entertainment without having to ask, "What can I do?" Making do for oneself can be pleasantly contagious, and an attribute a child will use and share into his adult life.

*   *   *

PLAYBOOK activities are organized according to the places where they are most likely to be built or played with, and suggestions follow about their use.

The division of projects into different play areas is by no means absolute. You will certainly find many of the activities listed for one play area to be just as suitable for another. Use your good judgment.

PLAYROOMS, BEDROOMS, FAMILY ROOMS, AND SCHOOL ROOMS are places where the child usually feels warmth, comfort, and happiness because he is familiar with them. These are "his" spaces—he knows where to find materials and tools and what the rules of play are. These spaces not only provide for play, but influence a child's taste and his sense of organization. They should be well-lit with plenty of storage space and places to hang things up. Nothing should be so terribly fragile or valuable that the child must be over-cautious or feel guilty about possible breakage. Don't be afraid to let kids make a mess duirng their play. As long as they are not destructive or wasteful, let them enjoy their projects fully. Spread out newspapers to protect a table or put aprons around the kids to protect them. Part of playing should be cleaning up, and if you explain this before you start, the child will expect to spend some time putting stuff back when he's through.

KITCHENS are especially private spaces for grown-ups, and letting children use them for their projects is a privilege. When allowed to use the kitchen, a child will identify with the parent and imitate what he does. It sometimes takes more effort to convince a child to go off and do something else when you are busy than to include him in your activities. Kids love to mix ingredients, stir stuff in a bowl, watch as their concoctions turn from batter to cake or from juice to popsicles. A child will almost always eat—or at least taste—what he has made himself. Don't assume, however, that the dish will be his favorite. He likes it mostly because he made it. You can expect kitchen play to be messy, so set the rules about cleanup beforehand. Although kids love to splash around in a sink full of soapsuds, that doesn't mean the dishes will ever get clean. Having fun is the main concern. Never allow rough play in the kitchen—there are just too many potentially dangerous tools and appliances about.

WORK ROOMS, TOOL ROOMS, BASE-MENTS, AND GARAGES are fascinating spaces for kids to tinker in or to use for a specific project. Besides the wonderful tools, there are almost always a few boxes and jars full of odd bits of hardware—screws, bolts, hinges, nails, draw-pulls, keys, locks, and strange things that you have probably long forgotten. Most younger children can only assist in the workshop but there's always something to hold, a bolt to be tightened with a wrench, or a

nail to be pounded in. Children feel very important when working with real tools (though for some reason they don't seem to like sanding.) Show the child how to work one tool at a time, explaining any potential dangers, then give him some scraps on which to try his hand (or he might use the tool on the house). No matter how well you explain, a child will not really understand until he has tried the tools himself. If you want the project to be the child's own, don't assist him. But don't expect or demand craftsmanship equal to your own. Young children cannot make long or straight cuts, or follow detailed instructions. But the *process* of building will be just as much fun as the completed project.

BACK YARDS, PORCHES, AND EMPTY LOTS. Playing outdoors is much more than getting exercise and fresh air. Children can make noise outdoors, sniff wonderful smells, discover "pets" under rocks, flirt with real and imagined dangers, roll down a hill, play street games, get around on a bike, build with sand, dirt, and rocks, climb trees, walls, and hills, collect pretty things, and sometimes just watch others at work or play. Outdoor play is spontaneous. Children can move freely without fear of breaking things and making a mess. Parents may need to keep an eye on the situation, but usually don't need to be involved beyond the organization of a given project. Playing outdoors offers children the freedom to explore and discover their own play spaces in trees, under steps, in alleyways, parks, construction sites, around a farm, at beaches, in streams, ponds, and puddles. Almost any out-of-sight place can be considered a play fort or a house. And wherever there's a place to climb, you'll find children up off the ground. Outdoor play is casual and often interlaced with small projects where scrap materials are plentiful—sticks, tires, building scraps, paper, stones, sand, and certain "lucky finds." Many projects take on a fresh new appeal by just being done outdoors.

CARS, TRAINS, PLANES, AND RESTAURANTS. Any time a child travels away from home, whether for an afternoon outing or the family vacation, the trip can be either an exciting adventure or a boring disappointment. Even if a child is eager about his planned trip, the anticipation usually won't sustain itself once the trip is underway. If the trip is going to be long you will eventually want the child to amuse himself.

Parents often bribe their children to be patient or quiet while they take care of their own business. One of the common bribes is the promise to buy the child a new toy. Wow! But the anticipation of the new possession creates the anxiety of wanting something to do *now*! And so the child soon asks, "How long before we go to the toy store?" "Can I get a Commander Corey Worm Locater?" When the bribe proves ineffective, on comes the threat of punishment which often ends in an unpleasant scolding situation.

The solution is to plan projects and activities in advance with the children in mind, and to let the child be part of the planning. If the trip is a new adventure, it is always good to have the child read (or be read to) about the type of excursion he is about to take. If travel is involved, let him pack his own bag of projects along with a few familiar possessions for security. On the way to your destination you can tell stories, play family word games, or sing

songs. Once you've arrived, the activities can continue, and you might look for new play materials. The unprinted side of a paper placemat from a restaurant is great to do paper and pencil games on while waiting for the food to be served. You might even start a collection of souvenirs.

Every PLAYBOOK project is prefaced with information, when helpful, that describes the use of the toy or game, gives some sidelights into its history, makes suggestions about planning the construction, and discusses the type of play you can expect. Children are sometimes conservative about their abilities and would rather ignore a project than possibly fail at doing it. Many parents have complained about a child ignoring a store-bought toy, but being perfectly content playing with the box it came in. There is nothing threatening about the empty box: it is probably a better toy than the one it contains because it can become anything the child's imagination will allow it to be. A great advantage to a child's inventiveness is his lack of preconceived ideas. A toy or project that may be played with in many different ways, as most of the PLAYBOOK projects can, is considered open-ended, and makes the best plaything. The toy must also be safe so that any potential dangers are recognized by the child. The older the child the more aware of danger he will be.

Most all of the projects list the materials and tools required for them. A material is considered anything that is consumed, and tools are those things that are necessary to do the construction but are not consumed. The tools required for most PLAYBOOK projects don't go beyond those found in most homes—scissors, pencil, hammer, pen knife, ruler, and various kitchen utensils. Don't use "play tools." A play hammer, scissors, or a saw just won't work as well (if at all) as real tools and become so frustrating as to discourage the entire project.

There is no particular order to the activities, so your child might thumb through the book or check the contents for a project that strikes his fancy. The listing of suggested minimum ages also helps decide which activities might be appropriate. A toy that is too simple to play with might bore a child in a short time, while one that is too difficult can lead to frustration and giving up. Before beginning a project, read it through completely to see if it meets the child's interest, if the materials are at hand, and how much of your time might be needed. If you have certain skills and interests, share them with your child. Children need to learn how to measure (although all measurements in the book have been kept to a minimum), to saw, glue, and draw, but try to work at the child's level of capability. Both of you know that the parent can do the "better" (neater) job, and your display of craftsmanship will not act as an example, but rather as a deterrent. To the child, your construction is "correct" and everything short of it is "wrong." Instead of craftsmanship, young children have a strong sense of workmanship: they are proud of their creations.

There are times when children run out of ideas for things to do and they approach you for help on some project. The parent's role in children's play is a delicate one. You should help the child organize his projects and answer any questions about how to build or use it. Young children who cannot read will, of course, need considerably more help. The child will follow your instructions by looking at the photograph and illustrations.

Don't underestimate a child's maturity and have him do projects that are too simple and don't hold his interest. Let the child do the work. Children learn more quickly from doing—and maybe doing wrong—than from being told how to do it. The parent should help the child through a tough spot when he can't manage on his own. But a child should never be "made" to do a project. You might suggest to your child that he look through PLAYBOOK and then let his own enthusiasm take over.

You may have little or nothing to do with building the projects after all, but the child may ask you to play it with him. By playing with your child you will get to know him a bit better. Many of the game activities can be played between parent and child, with both having an equal chance to win. If a child is losing at a game, help him formulate a new strategy, and he'll be eager to try again. Play with your child but don't play for him. A child likes to play because it's hard—easy play can soon become boring.

First and last, all PLAYBOOK activities are easy to do and they are *fun*. The fun comes in many ways, from selecting the project, gathering the materials and tools, doing the construction, playing with the toy, and then showing a friend how to do it.

PLAYROOMS, BEDROOMS, FAMILY ROOMS, SCHOOL ROOMS

ROOM WEAVING

ROOM WEAVING

A kid's room too often reflects his parent's tastes and standards for function and comfort. But a child's room should be his domain, a private and flexible space to help him develop self-expression and his own sense of culture. At a minimum, a kid's room should have accessible storage for clothes, toys, books, and materials; an uncluttered desk or table; open non-carpeted floor space for big indoor projects; a board for tacking things up; neutrally colored walls with art, posters, and project decorations that can easily be changed; and plenty of light. Even though a kid's room may be warm and happy, he still needs to be stimulated by small, frequent changes in his personal environment.

ROOM WEAVING is a simple project that quickly transforms a familiar room setting into an imaginative play-space. It might suggest a complex underground cave, a spider web (made by a dizzy spider), or maybe a thick jungle in the heart of Africa. Because the woven room is not bound to a recognizable reality, a kid can pretend and imagine it to be what he wants. A ROOM WEAVING can "stay up" until the child wants it down, or is obviously in the way of others. Parents may be relieved to know that what took hours or days to weave can be taken down in just a few minutes.

MATERIALS

string, yarn, ribbon, and the like
paper strips, cut-outs, or whatever
   you have to weave

CONSTRUCTION

There are no instructions on how to weave a room, only a few suggestions on how to get started. You will have to use your own imagination and ingenuity. Gather all the scrap string, yarn, and ribbon you can find. Tie smaller pieces together to make larger ones, the more the better. Start by attaching lengths of the various strings and things between "tie-on" places in the room—for example, from door knobs to window latches to closet rods to bedposts, and to legs of tables and chairs. The strings can be tied on with knots. After a few strings have been attached, you can begin tying strings between strings. You don't need to have a plan, just keep stringing and tying. When the weaving threads fill the room, you can weave in paper scraps and cut-outs or whatever you wish. A ROOM WEAVING doesn't have to be completed all at once, but can be added to as you like.

ROUND
CHECKERS

ROUND CHECKERS

Do you think you are a good checkers player? Well here's a different version of the game that really tests your skill. ROUND CHECKERS is not difficult to learn or play, but your moves must be carefully planned or the results can be disastrous—triple and quadruple jumps are quite common. Sometimes the game ends in a draw with both players down to one checker, chasing each other around the board with no chance for a jump.

The rules for ROUND CHECKERS are the same as for regular checkers. Players can move and jump their opponent's pieces only on the diagonal dark spaces. There are, however, these three exceptions to ROUND CHECKERS:

1. The checkers are set up for the round board as shown in the illustration.

2. Players can move their pieces forward *and* backward on the diagonal.

3. There are no kings.

MATERIALS

24 checkers (12 of each color), or make your
   own markers
a large sheet of cardboard or paper

TOOLS

scissors
dark colored crayon or marking pen
ruler

CONSTRUCTION

Draw a big circle on a large sheet of cardboard or paper. Draw a small circle in the center of the large circle. Now draw three more circles between the large and small circles so that all circles are about evenly spaced, see illustration. The circles must now be divided into sixteen segments. Draw a straight line through the circles to divide the board in half. Then draw another straight line through the circles to divide the board into four "pie" sections. Divide each of the sections with a straight diagonal line. The circles are now in eight pie sections. Divide these sections to make sixteen pie sections.

Using a crayon or marker, darken every other "square," staggering each row to create a "checkerboard." If you want, you can cut around the checkerboard to make one big circular board.

BUILDING WITH CARDS

BUILDING WITH CARDS

All play increases general coordination as well as providing an opportunity for imagination and creativity. But some play encourages manipulative skills especially. BUILDING WITH CARDS demands exacting "handsmanship" and concentration that at first seem difficult to achieve, but with growing self-confidence the child will develop a mastery of mechanical skills. Some children are, of course, naturally better coordinated than others, but when first learning to build with cards, most kids will need some help. Once the card structure is started, a child will find that he can easily add more cards to it, and be encouraged to perfect his skills to begin the next card building by himself. It isn't important that a kid build something specific—a factory, school, or skyscraper—and a parent should not suggest such things. Identical building units of a single shape encourage versatility and imaginative spacial relationships.

HOW TO DO IT

All you need for BUILDING WITH CARDS is one or more decks of playing cards.

The hardest part is starting the structure. You will quickly discover that it is much easier to build on a carpeted floor than on a smooth surface where the cards will slip. It might take a while to get the knack, but once you have learned to delicately balance two or three cards

26

against each other, it will seem quite easy. The illustration shows three basic constructions to get you started—from there the rest is up to you. You can build out across the floor, or your card buildings can go up two, three, or even four stories high. Do not become discouraged if your entire card building comes "crashing down." BUILDING WITH CARDS is a precarious art, and even a slight breeze or a jump on the floor can demolish an hour's building. But the idea of BUILDING WITH CARDS is not to see how long a structure will stand, but how big and complicated you can make it before it collapses. You have to decide if just "one more card" will be one card too many.

PIN BALL
MACHINE

PIN BALL MACHINE

PIN BALL MACHINE is a game of competition and skill. The degree of difficulty depends on the type of ball you use. It must be jiggled around the board! Small buttons or beans move a bit faster than pennies or dimes; small balls (BBs) are "lightenings" and only for the professional pin ball player.

The object of PIN BALL MACHINE is to see who can get the "ball" from start to finish without its falling off the playing board or going through one of the holes. Hold the PIN BALL MACHINE in both hands. Place your ball at "start," and tilt the playing board towards yourself until the ball begins to slide. Guide the ball by tilting and wiggling the playing board from side to side.

As soon as a player gets too good at a particular pin ball path, move the bobby pins and change the pattern of the obstacles.

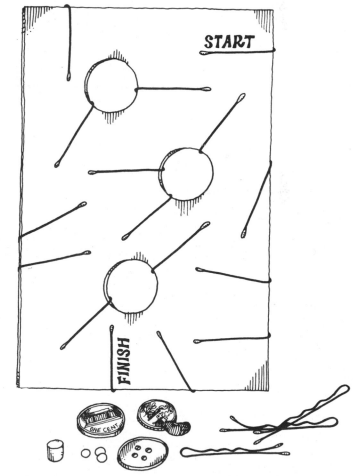

MATERIALS

square of heavy scrap cardboard (the back of a writing tablet works well)
bobby pins
waxed paper
balls—coins, buttons, beans, BBs, etc.

TOOLS

scissors
pencil

CONSTRUCTION

With scissors cut out one or more twenty-five or fifty-cent-sized holes in the cardboard. Rub a piece of waxed paper all over the surface of the cardboard. The more you rub, the more slippery the cardboard surface will be (and the faster and better the game). Slide bobby pins with the raised side up onto the cardboard from the board edges and from the edges of the cut holes. Try to make a winding path from one top corner of the board—mark it "start" with the pencil—to the bottom, which you mark "finish." Now try your skill with the chosen "balls."

FINGER MAZE CARDS

FINGER MAZE CARDS

A printed maze that you solve with a pencil is fun, but once you've done it, you've got to find or make another to do more. With FINGER MAZE CARDS you can create new and different mazes in a few minutes. In fact, if you have a deck of fifty maze cards you can make hundreds of different mazes. Some patterns will be quite easy to solve, some difficult, some impossible, but every one unique. The more maze cards you make and use, the more complex the maze becomes, and usually the more difficult to solve.

FINGER MAZE CARDS can be played as a solitaire game with the object being to find a path that gets you from start to finish, or two or more can compete to see who can solve the maze in the fastest time. Sometimes it is fun to see who can construct the most difficult maze pattern.

Good maze-solving strategy requires that you look ahead to see which path seems most favorable and which paths might lead to dead ends. You can use a simple trial-and-error method to find the correct path through the maze, but you will do better consistently if you use your mind and think the problem through. Some players like to trace the maze from both ends and hopefully meet somewhere in the middle.

For younger kids the FINGER MAZE CARDS can be used as an abstract puzzle offering endless possible designs. In this case, there is no correct way of working the cards. The only rule is to place them so that the lines connect to make pleasing patterns.

MATERIALS

thin cardboard (index cards, file folders, or heavy construction paper)

TOOLS

scissors
ruler
crayon or marking pen

CONSTRUCTION

Cut thin scrap cardboard into squares of the same size. Either measure out each square for cutting or make one good square to use as a pattern for the other cards. Any number of cards will do, but try to make at least fifty cards. Using a dark crayon or marking pen, copy the ten card patterns illustrated here onto the cards you have cut out. One of the patterns is blank. Try to have about the same number of

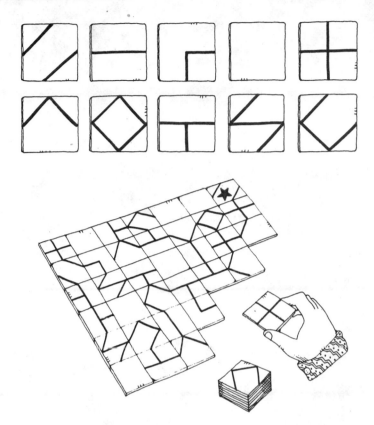

rows of cards with all cards and rows touching. (The overall shape of the maze is up to you.) If you start with fifty cards, you can make five rows of ten cards, or seven rows of seven cards (and have one card left over). See if you can follow the connecting lines from one dot card to the other without reaching a dead end. Use your finger to trace the path.

METHOD II. Start with one of the dot cards and lay out all the cards to form a maze. Your pattern can be tricky with a lot of dead ends, or a simple long winding one. End the maze with the other dot card. Challenge a friend to solve your maze.

cards for each pattern. Notice that all the pattern lines begin and end at the middle of an edge. This is so that the lines will connect or match up when the cards are placed together. Select any two of the FINGER MAZE CARDS you have made (except the blank cards) and mark a big dot on each one. One of the dot cards will represent the start position and the other dot card will be the finish.

HOW TO PLAY

METHOD I. Shuffle all the FINGER MAZE CARDS and deal them in order, face up. Make

SPIDER IN THE WEB

SPIDER IN THE WEB
(A Good Party Game for Younger Children)

Some children want to "boss" their own parties and make many of the planning decisions. Parties are an important event in growing up, and a child *should* participate in their planning. A kid usually knows whom he wants to invite, and what games his friends like to play; there are, however, a few important points a parent might keep in mind.

The success of a party does not depend on how elaborate the decorations and favors are, nor how stuffed with candy, ice cream, and cake the guests become. Children will be most pleased by having plenty of things to do. A parent should plan ahead and be prepared with many activities and games. The games selected should not require any special skills, so that everyone has the same chance to win. Prizes don't have to be given to game winners, but favors should go to everyone (just before going home).

SPIDER IN THE WEB is a fascinating party game which will help get the gathering going and "break the ice" for kids who might be bashful. Play begins with a large paper web with its giant "spider," all hung by a string. From a distance of four or five feet, the players feed the spider by tossing pipe cleaner bugs at the web, trying to make them stick. Each player starts with the same number of bugs and the one who sticks the most to the spider's web is the winner.

MATERIALS

sheet of heavy paper, notebook-sized or larger
 (an opened file folder or manila envelope is good)
string
button
pipe cleaners
dark colored scrap paper

TOOLS

scissors
pencil

CONSTRUCTION

Cut the paper into a square, if it is not already. Bring two corners of the square together and fold the paper on the diagonal to make a triangle, Figs. 1 and 2. Fold the triangle in half, Fig. 3, and then in half once again, Fig. 4. Notice that with each fold the triangle becomes smaller. One of the edges of the smaller triangle will be folded closed, and another edge will have an open double fold. Using scissors, cut several slits from the closed folded edge *almost* to the open folded edge, Fig. 5. The slits should be at least one inch apart across the entire side. Turn the triangle around, and now cut slits from the double open edge almost to the single folded edge. These slits should be made between the other cuts. Carefully unfold the triangle completely. Poke a small hole with a pencil point through the center of the square, and thread a length of string through the hole. Tie a large button to the underside end of the string and hang the paper square at a kid's eye level. Gently pull down on the edges of the paper square so it becomes a "web," see illustration. Fold a smaller piece of dark colored paper in half, and draw half the shape of a spider, Fig. 6. Cut out the spider, and put it in the web by weaving the spider's body and legs into the web's opening. Make the bugs by twisting two or three pipe cleaners together at the center, and bending the "legs" into hooks that will catch on the web. You might color part of each bug with felt markers so each player will have his own color bugs.

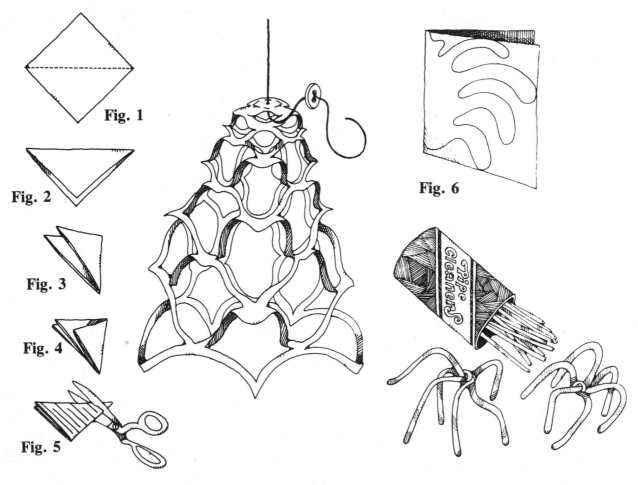

Fig. 1

Fig. 2

Fig. 3

Fig. 4

Fig. 5

Fig. 6

HAND SHADOWS

At some time every kid has discovered the amusement of playing with his own shadow and watching it mimic his own movements. Given the proper lighting and a plain wall, kids will be enchanted with their ability to create HAND SHADOW figures, and make the figures perform to their command. The variety of HAND SHADOWS that can be "thrown" onto a wall is limited only by imagination and the ability to figure out the proper hand and finger positions (that means patience helps).

Before trying to do the examples shown in the illustration, it might be best for a kid to experiment and throw any shadow pictures his hands shape, and then say what he has made. The illustrations show a few examples of hand and finger technique, but require a little practice to get right. Once the positions of the HAND SHADOWS have been mastered, a kid can animate the shadows by moving his hands and fingers to make wings flap, tails wag, ears wiggle, mouths talk or legs walk. Voices and sound effects may be added to complete the HAND SHADOW show.

To set up the light for HAND SHADOWS, place an unshaded lamp with a single bulb across the room from a blank section of wall. Of course, the room should be dark otherwise. Hold your hands a few feet from the wall, and adjust your arms and hands until the shadow pictures look the way you want. The further you move from the wall, the larger the shadow figures will become, but they won't be as sharp. Very often the proper light set-up already exists from an outside street light shining through your window, or a hallway light streaming in your room through a partially opened door. Once you have practiced the art of HAND SHADOWS, you will never be without an amusement to show your friends—or *your* children and grandchildren.

FINGERPRINTING

FINGERPRINTING

Did you know that you have something no one else in the world has? You have your very own fingerprints. Although they might not look much different from anyone else's at first, the pattern of ridges on the tops of your fingers is unique to you—no two persons' fingerprints are exactly the same. The pattern of your fingerprints never changes from the day you are born. Toe prints, foot prints, elbow prints and palm prints are some other body prints that are exclusively yours. But to identify a person, fingerprints are the most important. The Chinese once used fingerprints to sign letters. That was one sure way to stop someone from copying a signature.

Skin contains a small amount of "oil" to keep it soft. Therefore, every time someone touches an object with their bare fingers, they leave an invisible fingerprint. The invisible fingerprint is called a *latent* print, which you can make visible with a few simple materials. By finding the person whose finger matches the fingerprint, you can tell who has touched the object. Detectives often do this when trying to solve a crime.

Smooth surfaces are best for leaving fingerprints on. Although it is technically possible to find latent prints on paper, cloth, or other rough surfaces, clean glass or polished metal show fingerprints best. (Maybe your parents have already told you that—too many times.) If you have a magnifying lens, take a close look at your fingertips, and then look on a smooth surface for latent prints. Even with a magnifying lens some latent prints will be difficult to

see, if not completely invisible. To "develop" a latent print and then "lift" the print, you will need the following equipment:

MATERIALS

talcum powder
pencil
fine sandpaper

TOOLS

very soft feather
transparent tape

DEVELOPING AND LIFTING LATENT PRINTS

You must first develop a latent print to make it easy to see. Because a latent fingerprint contains skin oil, it is a bit sticky. If the surface you suspect a latent print to be on is dark in color, you can develop the print using talcum powder. Sprinkle a very small amount of talcum on the surface, and very gently brush the powder around with a soft feather. If the latent print is there, the talcum will stick to it and the print will become visible. If the surface is light in color, sandpaper the lead tip of a pencil point to

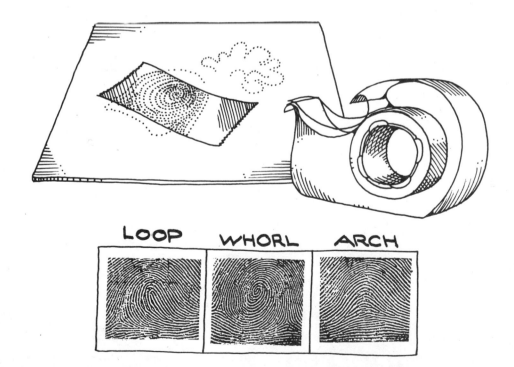

LOOP   WHORL   ARCH

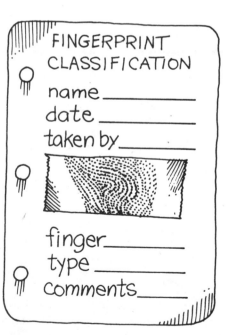

FINGERPRINT CLASSIFICATION
name_____
date_____
taken by_____

finger_____
type_____
comments_____

get fine graphite, and use this dark powder to develop the print.

Once the print is developed, you can easily save it by lifting the print with a piece of transparent tape. Cut a small piece of tape and place it directly on the developed print. Lift the tape and it will take the powder pattern of the print with it. To save the print, mount the tape on paper or cards. Use dark paper for talcum prints and white paper for graphite prints. Now if you want to play detective, you can do it the real way. Develop some latent prints around your room, and see if you can find whose fingers they match.

CLASSIFYING FINGERPRINTS

Although all fingerprints are different, there are a few fingerprint-type classifications. Three of the most common types are known as *loop*, *whorl* and *arch*. Look at the illustration of each type and compare them with your fingertips. How many loops, whorls and arches do you have? (Some fingerprints have double loops and other variations, but these are not common.) Under the fingerprints you have mounted on paper, write the proper classification—loop, whorl or arch. Include any other information, such as where you found the print and which finger the print came from (if you know). If you have the chance, visit your local police station and ask to see the fingerprint file and how a person's fingerprint is "taken" using ink. Now that you know how it's done, collecting fingerprints might make a good hobby.

CARDBOARD
MASKS

CARDBOARD MASKS

Mask making is quite an ancient art. For thousands of years masks have been used to create an illusion of mystery, comedy, majesty, and the supernatural. To some Africans, Eskimos, and American Indians, certain ceremonial masks were considered works of art. In Japan, metal masks were once used as face guards during battle. In Italy, hunters used masks to protect their faces from poking twigs and branches.

Today most masks are used just for fun. You may buy a mask for a special occasion, maybe a costume party, school play, or Halloween, but if you know how to make your own masks, they can be worn as an anytime play costume or disguise. A mask not only changes the wearer's appearance but it can instantly change his personality. Many shy kids will ramble on talking and mimicking freely because they feel hidden and secure behind a mask.

Special things must be considered when designing a mask. It must be comfortable to wear (not too hot and not too heavy), a mouth hole should be provided so that speech is easily heard, and vision should not be drastically blocked. If a kid can't see well through a mask, he is likely to trip or stumble on everything. And don't forget the mirror. You must look at yourself wearing a mask to understand the character you are going to be.

MATERIALS

cardboard boxes
yarn

TOOLS

pencil
scissors
crayons, markers, poster paint, etc.

CONSTRUCTION

Cut a long, rectangular-shaped piece from a corrugated box. If the box is large, one of the flaps will do. The long edge of the piece should go across the corrugations. Fold the piece in half back onto itself. If you open the piece to a "V" shape and place it over your face you will have the beginnings of a mask. With the piece held up against your face, try to "feel" where the eyeholes should be. Mark the spot on one side only with your finger, and then mark the spot with a pencil. Do the same to find where openings should be cut for the mouth and ears. You only have to mark the position on one side of the cardboard. With the mask folded so that its shape will be symmetrical, cut out holes and spaces for the eyes, mouth, and ears.

Fig. 1 shows a simple cutting pattern for a

first mask. The design of the face can be completed using crayons, felt markers, poster paint or collage. If you want a few ideas, just look in the mirror and twist up your own face. The theme of the mask is up to you—a sea creature, monster, clown, king, queen, or just any funny face. Punch a hole on either side of the mask at the rear, and tie a piece of yarn in one of the holes. Double-loop the yarn through the other hole so that it acts as an adjustable drawstring when fitting the mask. Put the CARDBOARD MASK over your face. The corrugated cardboard can be bent around your face for a better fit. Pull the drawstring tight so the mask won't slip down.

After making your first CARDBOARD MASK, you should experiment with cutting other shaped masks. A few suggestions are illustrated, but your imagination will work best for you.

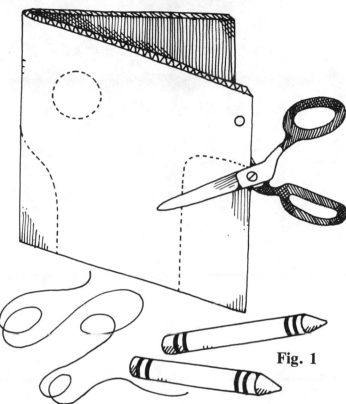

Fig. 1

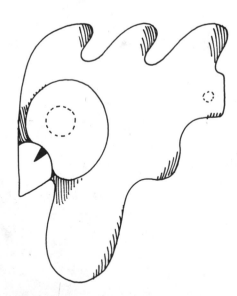

KALAH

KALAH

KALAH is an ancient game of skill—at least seven thousand years old—that has been played by many societies in many versions, and called by many names. A unique quality of KALAH is the varying degree of skill and strategy that can be used in play. A young kid and his equal opponent can start play with little conscious strategy. In successive playings, sophisticated strategies will gradually develop to make the games between children of different ages or parent and child truly competitive. (If a kid is too young to plan mental strategies and is consistently beaten at the game by a better player, he might consider the game too much work and quit.) As in all games requiring thought and strategy, KALAH should be played away from distractions—like the television.

MATERIALS

egg carton for a dozen eggs
36 or more markers (beans, pebbles, or buttons)

TOOLS

scissors

CONSTRUCTION

The playing board is made from the bottom of an empty carton for a dozen eggs. Either paper or plastic cartons will do. With scissors, cut off the carton lid and maybe save it for some other project. You need a minimum of thirty-six markers. Large, dry beans work well, but small pebbles, or buttons will also do. The markers do not have to be identical, so you can even mix different types.

HOW TO PLAY

In learning the rules, it will be helpful to refer to the illustration. KALAH is a game for two players. The players sit on opposite sides of the game board. The six "cups" on each player's side belong to him, and the table space to the *right* of each player's side of the board is his KALAH. The object of the game is to see which player can collect the most markers in his own KALAH.

The degree of difficulty of a game depends on the number of marker pieces in each cup at the start of play. For beginners, both players put three marker pieces in each of the six cups on

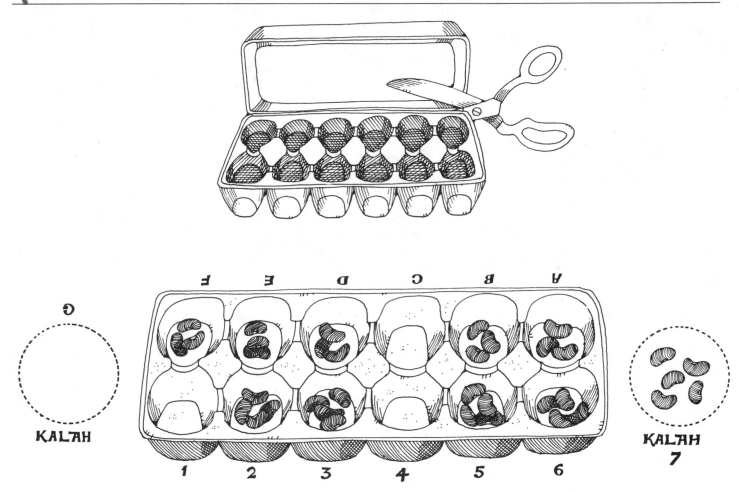

his side. One player is elected to move first, and picks up all the markers in any one of his six cups, and then puts those markers, one by one, in each cup, moving around the board to his right. If a player, in placing his markers, reaches the last cup on his side of the board and still has markers in his hand, he places one marker in his KALAH space and continues counterclockwise, placing markers one by one in his opponent's cups. However, a player never puts any markers in his opponent's KALAH.

There are two more rules that make the game interesting and help develop strategy. If the last marker of a player's move lands in his own KALAH, he gets another turn. If the last marker of a player's move lands in an empty cup on his own side of the board, he then takes all the markers out of his opponent's cup directly opposite his own empty cup. He puts these markers into his own KALAH, together with the marker used to capture them. That ends that player's move.

Here is an example of play: Player I picks up the three markers in cup number 4 and puts one marker into each cup moving to his right. The last marker lands in his own KALAH space (number 7). Player I, therefore, gets another turn. Player I now picks up all the markers in cup number 1 and puts them, one each, into the cups to his right. The last marker lands in his empty cup, number 4. Player I then captures the markers in Player II's cup C (opposite cup number 4) and puts those markers, along with his own capturing marker, in his own KALAH space (number 7). It is now Player II's turn.

This is a standard series of opening moves for a game starting with three markers in each cup.

The game is over when all six cups on either player's side are empty. Then, the player whose cups are not empty takes all the markers remaining in his own cups and puts them into his KALAH. The players then count up markers and the one with the most in his KALAH is the winner.

Later you might want to increase the difficulty of play and start with four, five, six or more markers in each cup.

BALL
AND
HAND
PUPPETS

BALL AND HAND PUPPETS

One of the best toys for play-acting is a puppet. With it any kid can "become" someone else and pretend to be somewhere else. When speaking through a puppet, a child will both imitate and act out real life situations—his own true feelings are often revealed in the creation of fantasy situations and imaginary friends and enemies. Many children who are normally "quiet" come alive when they can speak through a puppet. Not only does a child identify with the puppet character, but he has complete control over the puppet's world and therefore—temporarily—over reality. He decides what the puppet will do and say. With a few props and a story, a simple puppet performance can become a personal theater drama.

One of the easiest and best puppets to make is a BALL AND HAND PUPPET. All you need is a tennis ball for the head and a cloth napkin or handkerchief for the body. The most important part of any puppet is the face—its character and shape give the puppet its personality. By drawing on the tennis-ball head with felt-tipped pens, paint, or crayons, a kid can make his puppet a clown, a friendly animal, a not-so-friendly monster, or any character he likes. In a tennis-playing family, an entire theater company of BALL AND HAND PUPPETS might be created.

With a little practice a kid can easily learn how to make his puppets perform. He should move the head up and down when the puppet is speaking, and turn the head from side to side to have the puppet talk to other characters or people in the audience. Although the puppet head cannot change its expression, it can seem to change moods through head movements. A drooping head appears sad, and a quick, up-lifted head appears surprised. A child should also practice puppet hand movements so that the puppet can pick up and manipulate props.

A kid should learn to talk as the puppet character would by disguising his voice. Everyone will know who is really speaking, but the audience who can see only the puppet will easily accept the child's voice as that of the puppet. A puppet show should be prepared in advance. A script isn't necessary, but kids should plan to have the puppets do funny things. Lots of props should also be prepared.

Once a child has practiced, it's "show time," and a suitable theater and an audience will have to be found. An instant show might be put on from behind a sofa; to be more elaborate, the puppeteers can hide behind a sheet or blanket hung across a doorway, a few feet up from the floor, or draped over the back of a chair or small table.

MATERIALS

tennis ball
cloth handkerchief or napkin
rubber bands

TOOLS

penknife
felt markers or crayons

CONSTRUCTION

To make the puppet head, use a penknife to cut a hole in the tennis ball a bit larger than your index finger, Fig. 1. Decide what character the puppet will be, and decorate the tennis-ball head using felt markers or crayons. The line markings on the tennis ball might be used as the hairline.

The body of the puppet is made by draping a colorful cloth handkerchief or napkin over your hand which is held in the position shown in Fig. 2. Your index finger will be the puppet's neck, and your thumb and second finger will be the puppet's arms. The last two fingers should be folded into your palm. With the cloth draped over your hand, push your index finger into the hole in the tennis ball. Now slip a loose-fitting rubber band over the cloth around your thumb, and another rubber band over the second finger to better define the puppet's hands.

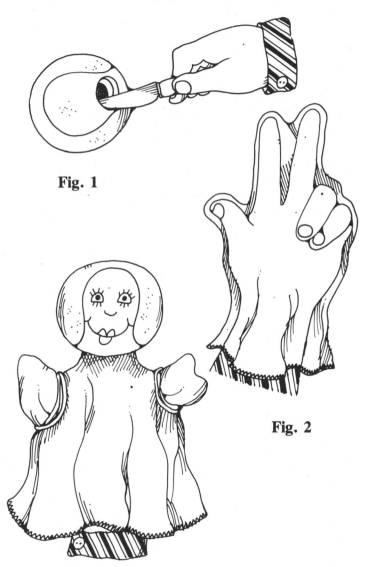

Fig. 1

Fig. 2

52

INSIDE
TENTS

INSIDE TENTS

Although a kid may have a room all to himself, he still needs a more private place in which to exercise his fantasies—a place protected from the intrusion of parents and brothers and sisters. Sometimes that private place can be a retreat behind the sofa, under a table or stairway, or in a secluded corner of a little-used room. But most kids would prefer to build their own private spaces, like an INSIDE TENT.

There are no specific instructions for making an INSIDE TENT. All that is necessary is a few sheets and blankets for draping, and some rubber bands or string to fasten the chosen material to chair backs, upside-down table legs, and beds. A few large safety pins can help to shape the tent. But probably the most important thing is permitting the child use of a space where he can set up his tent and keep it up for a few days. In time, the tent will probably get a front and back "door," or maybe a second tent room will be added. Favorite toys and other treasures will be brought into the tent as well as a pillow to make a sleeping space and some food to snack on. Some kids will want to spend the night in their INSIDE TENT. If you are a camping family, inside tenting is great "overnight" preparation for younger children. If a child has already been camping or even just talked about it, the play tent situation will probably include pretend fishing, hunting, hiking, a

campfire, and cooking. Whatever the theme of the space and the make-believe fantasies, INSIDE TENTS is an instant activity that grows into lots of adventure and learning play.

PAPER HATS

PAPER HATS

Because you can often tell the kind of work someone does by the hat he wears, you can pretend to be that someone by just wearing his hat. Maybe you would like to be a police-woman, postman, train conductor, nurse, engineer, construction worker, hunter, detective, cowboy, pilot, sea captain, or soldier. Fold and decorate a PAPER HAT and be anyone you would like. Or, if you point up the ends of the PAPER HAT to make ears and wear the hat sideways, you can pretend to be a fox, rabbit, horse, mouse, or any animal with pokey ears. A PAPER HAT can even be used as an emergency rain cap or a painter's hat to keep drips out of your hair. Once you learn to construct PAPER HATS, you will be able to make a hat anywhere—right on the spot—by just folding a sheet of newspaper. And "one size fits all"!

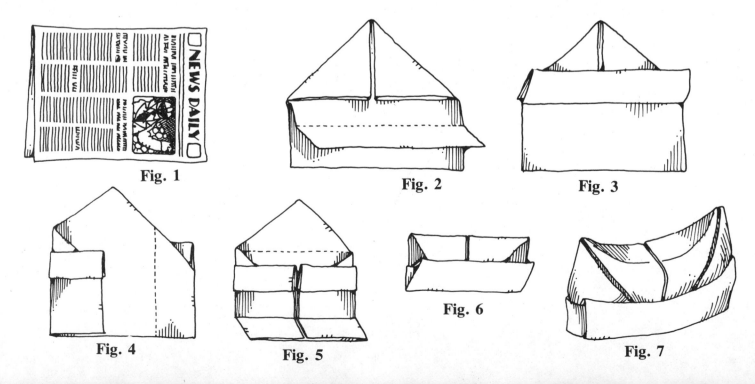

Fig. 1

Fig. 2

Fig. 3

Fig. 4

Fig. 5

Fig. 6

Fig. 7

CONSTRUCTION

All you need is a double-page newspaper sheet. Fold the newspaper to a one-page size, Fig. 1. Position the newspaper so that the open end is at the bottom. Fold both upper corners over so that they meet in the center of the page, and fold up the top page so that it meets the two upper folds, Fig. 2. Crease all the folds well. Fold the top sheet over again so that it covers the bottom of the upper folds, and crease, Fig. 3. Now, turn the paper construction over. Fold one side in to the middle, Fig. 4, and then fold the other side in. (At this step in the construction you may alter the hat size a bit. To make a larger fitting hat, fold the two ends in—but not all the way—to the center. Crease the folds well.) Fold the bottom sheet up to meet the top folds as you did on the other side and crease, Fig. 5. Now slightly unfold the bottom sheet and tuck it into the "hat band," bottom of Fig. 6. Be careful not to tear the newspaper while tucking in the flap.

The paper hat is almost complete. If you opened the hat to wear now, it would have a pointed cone on top. You can fold down the point and also tuck it into the hat band, Fig. 6, to make a cap, Fig. 7. Or fold one or both corner points down into the hat band to make other style hats. It's up to you to decorate your PAPER HATS with words, badges, or symbols to tell what kind of worker you will pretend to be.

WIG OF YARN

WIG OF YARN

Did you ever wonder what you would look like with long, yellow pigtails, or maybe big orange bunches of hair with purple bows? No? Well, did you ever want to pretend to be a glamorous movie star, a long-haired rock musician, or a wild-haired "mad scientist?" Hair "tells the story," and your dress-up costume won't really be complete until you have made and worn an outrageous WIG OF YARN. (Sometimes the wig is all the costume you need.) A wig of yarn can be almost any style or color, and it is a costume you can make yourself without cutting and sewing fabric. You should, however, have a friend to help you "fix" and groom your wig, and to tell you how funny you look.

MATERIALS

heavy yarn (for quantity, see below)

TOOLS

scissors
ruler

CONSTRUCTION

You will need to decide how long you want your WIG OF YARN to be. A very short wig style will require one skein of yarn cut into two-foot long strands. A medium-length wig requires two skeins of yarn cut into three-foot strands, and for a long wig (for braiding or bunches) you will need three skeins of yarn cut into four-foot lengths. A parent may have some leftover yarn from a knitting project that you can use, but if not you can buy inexpensive rug yarn—it's heavy and comes in many bright colors.

Measure and cut all the yarn to the middle of

a bunch of three strands, Fig. 1. Now, reversing the procedure, tie a bunch of three strands, at the middle, to the single strand, and slide the knot down the single strand to the first bunch, Fig. 2. Continue to add strands in bunches of three to the single strand. When all the yarn has been used, tie off the single strand with a good knot. Adjust the wig on your head with the "part"—the single strand—at the middle of your head. A wig of yarn can be groomed into different styles just like real hair. Have a friend help. For a plain wig style, just trim the ends with scissors. If you are going to make pigtails or bunches, do them first, tie with a ribbon bow, and then trim the ends with scissors. Now look at yourself in a mirror and, if you have the nerve, wear your beautiful hair in public!

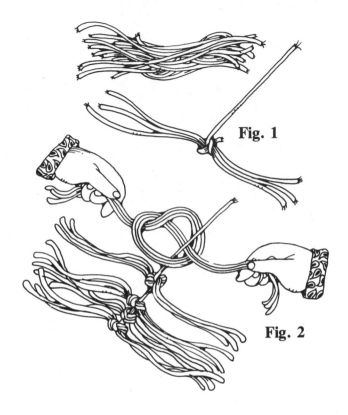

Fig. 1

Fig. 2

GOD'S
EYE
WEAVING

GOD'S EYE WEAVING

To the wise Pueblo and Mexican Indians, the GOD'S EYE was a sacred decoration that brought good fortune, luck, health, and long life. The colorful weaving represented the "eye of God" and all His good powers. Even today, GOD'S EYES are believed to bring happiness and good luck—and everyone can use some of each. GOD'S EYES can be made in many designs and shapes and can be hung on walls, in windows or as mobiles; worn as a hair ornament and other types of jewelry; or carried as "good luck" charms if sufficiently small. GOD'S EYE weaving is easily learned by kids, and a simple weaving can be completed quite quickly. Once you have mastered the technique, there are endless stick designs and color patterns you might try. Good luck!

MATERIALS

two sticks the same size: ice cream sticks, twigs, cotton swabs, plastic stirrers, chopsticks, flat toothpicks, pick-up sticks, Tinkertoy rods, pencils, etc.
yarn, thread, or string

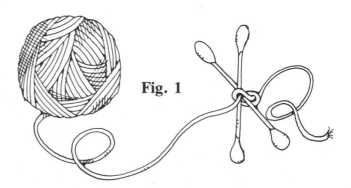

Fig. 1

TOOLS

scissors

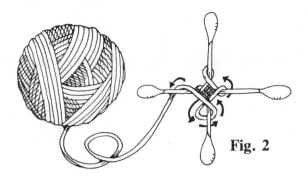

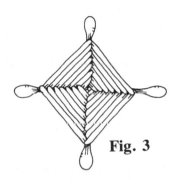

Fig. 2

Fig. 3

other hand. Weave the yarn over one leg of the skeleton, then under, around and over the same leg, Fig. 2. Go to the next leg and weave around it the same way—over the leg, under, around, and over. After each weave around a leg, push the weave towards the center of the cross to make it snug. Continue around the skeleton, weaving the second row the same way, and so on. You will soon develop a good rhythm for weaving, and after a few rows will see the triangular "eye" appearing. You can weave the entire skeleton with the same yarn, or change yarns by knotting the two yarn ends together. Changing colors often makes the designs more exciting. Finish off the GOD'S EYE by tying the end of the yarn around a leg of the skeleton. The "good" side of the weaving will be smooth, and the back side show the crossed sticks, Fig. 3.

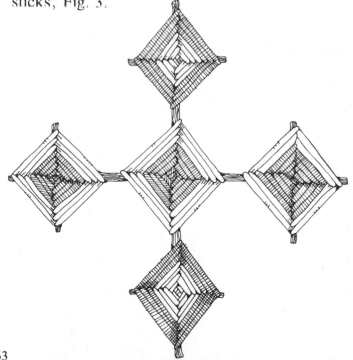

CONSTRUCTION

Select two sticks the same size and put them together to form a cross, with all four "arms" equal. This is the "skeleton" of the GOD'S EYE. Take one end of the yarn or string you want to start with, and tie it around the center of the crossed sticks to tie them together, Fig. 1. Make the knot tight so the sticks are not wobbly.

There are many ways to weave a GOD'S EYE, but the basic weave is called the front wrap. Hold the skeleton in one hand keeping the sticks crossed, and hold the yarn in your

PAPER CUP DOMES

PAPER CUP DOMES

A kid can make a toy from—or play with—most discards. Much of what is thrown away can become valuable additions to a child's scrap box—paper, tubes, egg and milk cartons, fabric remnants, stickers that come in mailings, bags, cardboard boxes, and paper cups. Often there are discards that can be brought home from the office or shop—computer paper, nuts and bolts, reject parts, and used paper cups from the water cooler. Indeed, until we stop using our resources for consumable products, there will always be a ready supply of discards that might as well have a second life as a toy.

PAPER CUP DOMES are built from discarded paper drinking cups and some glue. The project requires one hundred or more cups, but constructions using fewer cups can be exciting. Twelve or twenty cups fastened together will make an interesting desk-top organizer, or a place to keep collections of special objects. If a kid is really ambitious, he can build a complete sphere and with some help, turn it into a lamp. But whatever is made, the real fun of PAPER CUP DOMES is in the building.

MATERIALS

lots of used paper drinking cups, all the same
   size and type
glue (or paper clips or staples)

TOOLS

spring clothespins

CONSTRUCTION

There are three methods for building PAPER

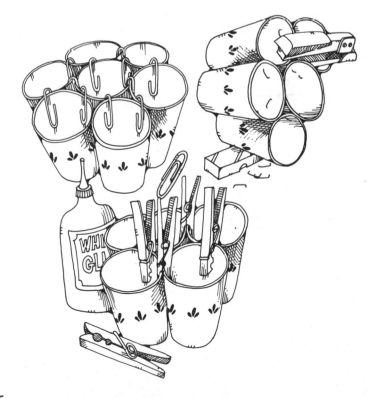

65

CUP DOMES. If you want to make a permanent construction, it's best to glue the cups together using spring clothespins to hold the cups in place while the glue dries. But if glue is used, the cups *cannot* be the type coated with wax or plastic because then the glue won't hold. You can connect wax and plastic coated cups—or even plain paper cups—by one of two other methods. The cups can be stapled together using a small hand stapler, or for less permanent constructions, regular paper clips will do. Using the fastening method of your choice, start with one cup, and continue to affix one cup at a time to it until your construction is complete, see illustration. Do not try to build separate groups of cups and then fasten the sections together. It doesn't work well. Your project will be complete whenever you run out of materials, or time.

STRAW AND CLIP BUILDING

STRAW AND CLIP BUILDING

Drinking straws are an ideal building unit to make your own construction set. Straws are either inexpensive to buy, or free at many hamburger restaurants. But if you do collect straws from restaurants, don't be piggish. Drinking straws come in a few different sizes and types—paper, plastic, skinny, fat, extra-long, or regular length. For STRAW AND CLIP BUILDING you can use any type of fat straws (the common type you are most familiar with). The length of the straw does not matter because you can cut the straw with scissors to any length you want.

MATERIALS

straws
string or pipe cleaners or paper clips (or all
   three)

CONSTRUCTION

There are three different ways to connect drinking straws for building. The most difficult straw constructions, but the most permanent, are made by connecting the straws together with string. Stick the string in one end of the straw and suck on the other end until the string comes through. Thread three straws on a string,

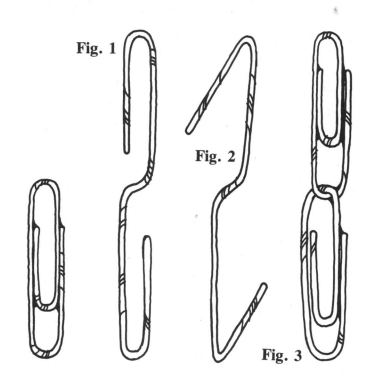

Fig. 1

Fig. 2

Fig. 3

then pull together and tie the string ends to make a triangle. The triangle is the only basic straw-and-string shape that will stay rigid enough for building. Add a second straw triangle to the first and so on.

Another method of building with straws is to use pipe cleaners as connectors. Push a pipe cleaner half-way into the end of one straw. Slip another straw over the other end of the pipe cleaner. If the fit is too loose, double up the pipe cleaner before inserting it in the straw. Bend the pipe cleaner where the straws meet to create the shape you want and continue building the same way.

The best method of building with drinking straws is to use common paper clips as connectors. To connect two straws, open a paper clip, Fig. 1, and slightly bend out each of the two loop ends, Fig. 2. This makes the paper clip fit inside the straw tightly. Bend the paper clip at the middle to any angle you want, then slip a drinking straw over each end of the clip. Con-

tinue adding straws with paper clips in the same way. To build structures it will be necessary to fit more than one clip into a straw end. Three clips in a straw is okay, more might make the straw crack. Because the paper clips are rigid, you can build in any shape or direction you want. You can also chain two paper clips together to make a flexible joint between two straws, Fig. 3. After connecting four or five straws, your building will begin to take some shape. Try building a tall tower to stand on the floor, or maybe a model version of the TUBE DOME, page 123. Whatever type of structure you build, you can always add on a new section. If you like, the STRAW AND CLIP BUILDING can be taken apart, and all the straws and clip connectors saved in a shoe box for another construction some other day.

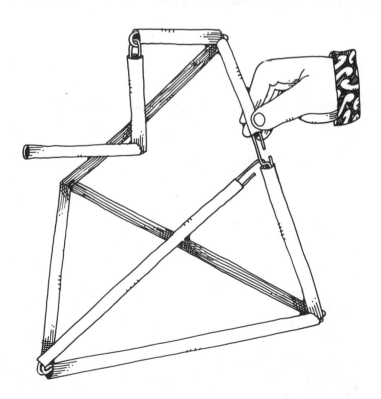

BALLOON ROCKET

BALLOON ROCKET

Every kid knows that if you blow up a balloon and let it go, the balloon will rocket crazily around the room. It would be much more fun, however, if you could control the balloon's flight to go smooth, straight, and farther. With a little know-how and lots of trial and error, a BALLOON ROCKET will perform quite well. But balloons have a way of suddenly bursting and sometimes, just when you have adjusted and perfected your BALLOON ROCKET, it will pop and you have to "break in" a new, unpredictable balloon. Have a contest with yourself and see how far, how high, and how accurately you can fly your BALLOON ROCKET—then maybe have a contest with a friend.

MATERIALS

plastic drinking straw
long, straight balloons
rubber band
thin scrap of cardboard (postcards are perfect)

TOOLS

scissors
pencil

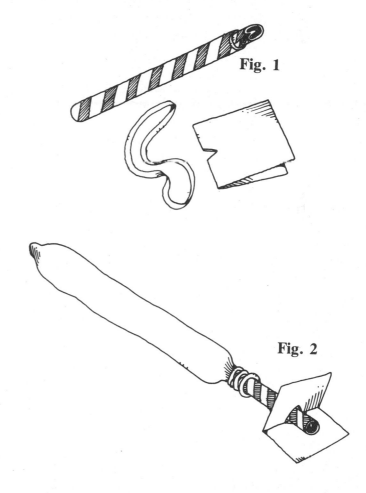

Fig. 1

Fig. 2

CONSTRUCTION

Cut a plastic drinking straw in half, and push one piece inside the other. It's easy to do if you first pinch and then fold one straw end slightly before inserting it in the other, Fig. 1. Now select a long, straight balloon (rather than a round one) and insert the double straw a few inches into the balloon neck opening. Wrap a rubber band around the neck of the balloon several times to hold the straw firmly in place and to make a good air seal around the straw. Make the BALLOON ROCKET'S stabilizer fin by cutting out a rectangular piece of thin cardboard from a postcard or file folder. Fold the cardboard piece in half and cut a small notch in the middle of the folded edge to allow the straw to slip through snugly. Slip the stabilizer fin over the end of the straw just far enough so that it won't slip off, Fig. 2. If the fin is loose, use a small piece of tape to hold it in place.

You are ready for the first test BALLOON ROCKET launch. Blow up the balloon through the straw until it is completely full. To keep the air from escaping while you handle the BALLOON ROCKET, pinch the end of the straw or hold your finger over it. Aim the rocket up at a slight angle and let it go.

You will probably have to experiment with the size and shape of the fin. If the BALLOON ROCKET just zooms around like a plain balloon, you might need a larger stabilizer fin. And if the rocket doesn't seem to go anywhere, the balloon could be too small or the fin too large. You can also control to some degree the rate of air blasting out of the straw to get a longer or quicker flight. Pinch the end of the straw to reduce the rocket's power or poke the straw hole open with a pencil point to increase the rocket's thrust.

When you have experimented and worked out the problems of making a smooth, far- and high-flying BALLOON ROCKET, try some new ways of launching the rocket. Blast off straight up for altitude, or try to land the rocket on a table. But do watch out for the big "pop."

GAME KIT

GAME KIT

Nearly all board games of chance for young kids are played the same way. Each player in turn throws the dice or flicks a spinner to see how many spaces he can move, and then the player lands on a space that is either a reward ("Take another turn"), a penalty ("Go back to start"), or just a "safe" space. The themes of the games are different—names like "Chase the Frog," "Ecology Clean-up," or maybe "Monster Madness"—but they are all usually played the same way. With a GAME KIT, you create a game board that can be used for any number of different games. You choose your own theme. And if you make up your own game board you can also make up your own rules. Just remember that all players must understand and play by the same rules. Now try to *win* at your own game.

MATERIALS

plain cards or paper
marker pieces—buttons, coins, pebbles, etc.

TOOLS

scissors
felt markers or crayons

CONSTRUCTION

There are several typical spaces on a game board that represent rewards and penalties. Here are a few, but you should make up some of your own.

Take another turn
Move ahead 1 (2 or 3) spaces
Safe
Go back to start
Lose one turn
Go back 1 (2 or 3) spaces

Use at least twenty-five cards or scraps of paper, and write a penalty or reward on each one with a felt marker or crayon. You can repeat each penalty or reward as many times as you like, but do try to have about the same number of penalties as rewards. Also make one "Start" and one "Finish" card. The more cards you make, the longer the game playing will be.

You can use a single die or a spinner to determine the number of spaces a player moves. To make a spinner, cut out a six-sided shape from a scrap of cardboard and write numbers for moves on each edge—1, 2, and 3—each written twice works well. Stick a stubby-pointed pencil through the center and give it a spin. The side against which the spinner falls indicates the number of moves.

Now collect a different game marker for each player. Anything will do, but you might find buttons, coins, or pebbles handy.

HOW TO PLAY

There are different ways you can lay out or "make" the game board. For a real game of chance, shuffle all the penalty and reward cards (except the "Start" and "Finish" cards) and lay them out in order. Then place the Start card at one end of the chain and the Finish card at the other end.

You can also arrange the card spaces in any order you want. You might put the terrible penalties near the end of the game so all players will dread the thought of having to move back or lose a turn just when they thought that the game was won. Each time you play, rearrange the cards to make a different game board.

All players place their markers on the Start space and in turn throw the die or spin the spinner to determine how many spaces they move. A player must follow the reward or penalty of the space he lands on. Sometimes you can be fooled and what seems like a reward can become a penalty. Suppose the space you land on says "Go ahead 3 spaces" but when you move ahead you land on a space that says "Go back to start!" That is what can happen in a game of chance.

PICTURE PRINTING

PICTURE PRINTING

Did you ever try printing your own newspaper? At some time or other, every kid wants to publish his own newspaper and do all the printing. Maybe you made only one copy—and tried to sell it to a relative. The enthusiasm may last through the first issue only or it might signal the beginning of an interest in journalism. However, all first attempts at printing by kids are delightfully rough. Headlines are usually made in large printed capitals. The copy is either hand-printed or typed, and the illustrations are of the stick-figure variety.

An easy way to polish up your second and all future issues is to include PICTURE PRINTING. In PICTURE PRINTING you can "lift" pictures and printing from newspapers and magazines, black-and-white or color, and transfer them to your paper. The original picture is not destroyed in any way. You can also "lift" headline words and sentences, then rearrange them to make your own newspaper headlines. You can lift pictures from the comic section and add them to your own stories.

Using another form of PICTURE PRINTING, the Carbon Paper Press, you can do carbon rubbings of things like leaves, coins, keys, string and rubber-band designs. The carbon pictures are not detailed copies like the wax pictures, but the texture and designs you get from them can be even more interesting. Whether you do PICTURE PRINTING to make a newspaper or print posters, greeting cards, or invitations, you will find that it is the process of printing itself that is the most fun of all.

WAX PICTURES

MATERIALS

newspapers and magazines
white wax candle
white paper

TOOLS

spoon

HOW TO DO IT

Look through a newspaper or magazine to find a picture or anything printed that you want to lift and transfer onto a sheet of white paper. Although the printing can be black-and-white or color, you will get the best results if the newspaper or magazine is not very old. Rub the candle all over one side of a sheet of white paper to get a thin wax coating. If you only want to lift a small picture or anything less than the full size of the white sheet, coat the white sheet with wax only where you want the transfer picture to be. Put the white paper sheet over the picture or printing you want to transfer, with the waxy side down against the picture. Work on a flat, smooth surface. Hold the two pieces of paper down with one hand so that they don't slip, and rub the back of the white paper with the rounded bowl of a spoon. Rub fast and with some pressure. Lift away the white paper sheet, and you will see an exact transfer of the picture you were copying. There's only one problem—everything in your copy picture will be in reverse. If there are no words in the picture, you may want to use it as it is, but you can place another white sheet of paper over the transfer picture (no additional waxing required), rub it with the spoon, and you will get a "right way" version of the picture just like the original. However, each time you transfer the same picture, it will get a bit lighter in tone. You can cut apart the words and pictures you like, and paste them up in any way you like on another paper sheet.

CARBON PAPER PRESS

MATERIALS

carbon paper
white paper
cardboard

TOOLS

spoon or rolling pin
scissors

HOW TO DO IT

Rubbings from basically flat textured surfaces such as a leaf or coins can be made with the use of a Carbon Paper Press. To build the press, make a paper andwich with three kinds of paper all cut to the same size (if they are not already the standard 8½ x 11-inch size). First put down a sheet of cardboard. The cardboard back of a paper tablet is fine. On top of the cardboard, put a sheet of carbon paper—carbon side up—and then on top of the carbon paper, place the paper sheet that will receive the printed picture. Place the object you wish to transfer between the bottom cardboard and the uncoated side of the carbon paper. Rub the top paper sheet with the smooth bowl of a spoon or roll it with a rolling pin. Be sure to press down hard. Remove the top paper sheet and turn it over to see the carbon paper picture. Unlike WAX PICTURES, carbon paper pictures do not come out in reverse. Because there will probably be many carbon marks around the picture rubbing, you can cut the picture out around its outline and mount it.

To set up the Carbon Paper Press again, just put a new paper sheet on top of the carbon paper and cardboard and you are ready to print again. Continue to use the same piece of carbon paper until it tears or begins to make weak-toned pictures.

KITCHENS, GALLEYS, PANTRIES, MESS HALLS

BOTTLE
SANDWICHES

BOTTLE SANDWICHES

Here are projects which will make use of "waste" food like table scraps, bits of stale cereal left in the box, or those few beans in the bottom of the bag. BOTTLE SANDWICHES are in fact collections of either dry food scraps or liquids put into large bottles. Surprisingly, the completed project can be a decorative work of art. Playing with food can be fun, but you should never play with food during meals.

MATERIALS

dry food scraps such as bread, cracker and cookie crumbs; any kind of bean; corn kernels or other seeds; any cereal, etc.
liquids such as water, milk, cooking oil, honey, ketchup, gravy, mustard, salad dressing, coffee, ink, or other leftovers
large empty clear bottles

TOOLS

measuring cup
funnel
spoons

CONSTRUCTION

Decide to make either a dry or a liquid

BOTTLE SANDWICH, but do not try to mix liquid and dry ingredients. You would just get smelly gook.

DRY BOTTLE SANDWICHES are a bit easier and less messy to make. Rinse and clean off any labels from a large empty clear bottle. Organize the dry food you have gathered into separate groups. For example, put all the white beans together in one place, the yellow crumbs in another, and the oat cereal in a third. Start with one group of food and, either piece-by-piece or by spoonfuls, fill the bottle about one inch deep. Then take food of a contrasting color or texture and fill the bottle a little more. You decide how much you want to put in of any one ingredient, but remember that you want to create a pattern with different layers of food. You don't have to complete the BOTTLE SANDWICH all at once. Save dry food scraps, and add them to the bottle as you gather them to make other layers of the sandwich.

LIQUID BOTTLE SANDWICHES do not always turn out as pretty as DRY BOTTLE SANDWICHES, but the messing around leads to some interesting experiments. Many liquids change when mixed with other liquids. Some liquids form *solutions*—a mixture in which two or more liquids blend evenly with each other like milk and water. Some liquids do not mix at all and form *suspensions*, like oil and water. In a suspension, one of the liquids settles to the bottom and the other remains on top. That is why many bottles of food say "shake well before using" on their labels. Using a measuring cup or funnel if the neck of your bottle is narrow, build layers of different types of liquids for your BOTTLE SANDWICH. Watch what happens as you pour different liquids onto each other. Look for solutions and suspensions. If the sandwich ends up yucky, pour it out and try again using different ingredients. Some BOTTLE SANDWICHES look great, and you will want to display them.

NOODLE JEWELRY AND BUTTON RINGS

NOODLE JEWELRY AND BUTTON RINGS

One of the most fun and imaginative forms of play for kids is "dressing up." A costume can become quite elaborate and lead directly to play dramas. A girl wearing a large skirt (pinned to fit), a fancy hat, a pocketbook, clackety-high-heel shoes, pretend jewelry, and maybe a spot of make-up is fantasizing the role she is going to play as a grown-up. Not a role, necessarily, but rather the attitude of the adults she is familiar with.

Watching a child mimic the adult world around him can often be amusing, but it is also one of the best times to understand how a kid perceives his family and those experiences that have influenced him. What is real and what is imaginary to a child is often confused. Sometimes the purpose of make-believe play is quite apparent, and a child will try to work out his own problems in play fantasy. Quiet children can sometimes become quite assertive in dress-up play. Although a child can only pretend about what he has seen or experienced, a parent can also suggest dress-up play and drama that will prepare a child for a new event that is going to happen—a trip to the hospital or a stay with a relative.

Dress-up to a preschool child can require nothing more than a special hat or a badge, but the older the kid, the more costume he will want, and the more attention paid to details (an important essential for dress-up play is a large mirror so the child can view himself). A well-equipped dress-up box is the secret to good inventive costumes, and will be used for many years. A large cardboard box can be used or a specific drawer may be assigned to be stocked with discarded clothing and materials. Here are some suggestions:

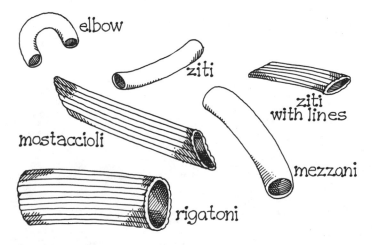

elbow

ziti

ziti with lines

mostaccioli

mezzani

rigatoni

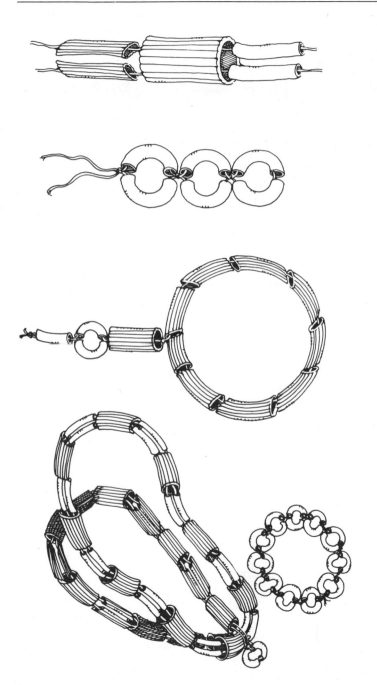

hats	ties	pocketbooks
shoes	scarves	material scraps
shirts	dresses	fancy trimmings
gloves	feathers	safety pins
slips	shopping bags	simple make-up
towels	vests	play jewelry

NOODLE JEWELRY AND BUTTON RINGS are simple dress-up accessories that kids can wear every day or may be added to a dress-up costume. **NOODLE JEWELRY** is a bit fragile, and it is a good idea to keep it in a "jewelry shoe box."

MATERIALS   TOOLS

hollow, dry noodles   scissors
string   crayons or felt markers
buttons
pipe cleaners

CONSTRUCTION

NOODLE JEWELRY can be strung in many designs and sizes depending on the kind of noodles you have and the jewelry you want to make. The illustrations show a few different types of common noodles that make good jewelry and a few ways to string them together. You might make a long necklace from two or more types of noodles, or a fancy bracelet by stringing many small noodles in a decorative pattern. Once you get started making NOO-DLE JEWELRY, you will have no trouble inventing your own designs. As an added touch, you can color some of the noodles with crayon or felt marker.

BUTTON RINGS are quite stylish and can be made quickly. Select large buttons with large holes. Push a pipe cleaner through two button holes and then bend the pipe cleaner around to fit your finger. Some fancy buttons only have a single wire loop on the underside. With these, push the pipe cleaner through the loop and around your finger two or three times so the ring won't be floppy.

IRON-ONS

IRON-ONS

The idea behind IRON-ONS is so simple— and it really works. Any crayon drawing you make can be permanently transferred to cloth using a hot clothes iron. Or, you can crayon directly onto cloth and then iron the drawing into the fabric. For your design you might copy a picture, draw your own, write your name in fancy letters, think up a funny phrase, or just create colorful patterns. Your drawings can be ironed on to T-shirts, or on plain cloth to make banners, wall hangings, placemats, flags, or any sewing project you can do. Once the crayon has been ironed in, the cloth may be washed repeatedly in cold or warm water without running or fading.

MATERIALS

TOOLS

crayons
cloth

clothes iron

THE DETAILS

Decide what your crayon project is going to be and organize your materials. Make your drawing either directly onto the cloth or onto a plain piece of paper. But remember, if you are going to transfer a drawing from paper to cloth the result will be in reverse. Either way, be sure to press hard on the crayons so that your colors go deep. Light crayon drawings just do not transfer well.

The ironing should be done, or at least supervised, by an adult. Set the iron temperature selector for the type of fabric you are applying the drawing to. Place the drawing on the cloth, crayon side down, or if you have crayoned directly onto the cloth, leave it crayon side up. Iron slowly over the drawing, giving the crayon enough heat to melt and impregnate the cloth. As the crayon melts, the colors will become a bit brighter and possibly spread a little. (You will also find that your drawing is still on the paper.) Remove the drawing, and your IRON-ON is complete. If any crayon remains on the iron, wipe it away with a wad of paper toweling while the iron is still warm.

HEARTS
AND
FLOWERS

HEARTS AND FLOWERS

HEARTS AND FLOWERS is a craft project using shaped pipe cleaners dipped into a thick, colorful goo. When the pipe cleaner shapes have dried, the result is small imitation "stained glass" objects which can be used as play jewelry, window decorations, or a lovely bouquet in a paper-cup vase. However, there are a few hints for keeping the project orderly and fun.

Almost any art project needs organization to ensure its success and to avoid making a mess. HEARTS AND FLOWERS is not necessarily an untidy project, but it does involve materials that if not used properly could create a difficult clean-up job. The parent must help organize the project—at least the first time. Kids should be pleasantly instructed in the use of project materials and told why protecting furniture, floors, and themselves from sloppy materials is important. A parent might assist and advise, but the child should clearly understand at the onset that part of the project is cleaning up. Parents should be certain that enough time is left for clean-up before the child is scheduled to do something else. Once a kid understands the conditions of working and playing with messy materials, he will repeat the process in a neat fashion each time.

MATERIALS

old newspapers
liquid white glue
food coloring
pipe cleaners
scrap of plastic foam

TOOLS

spoon
small bowl

CONSTRUCTION

Get together all the materials and tools, and prepare the work surface by protecting it with a few layers of old newspaper. It's also a good idea to wear a painting smock or an old shirt to protect yourself. Pour the liquid white glue into the bowl to a depth of at least one-half inch. Choose a food color—or a combination of colors—and add as much coloring as necessary (drop by drop) to make a pretty and bright mixture. Use a spoon to blend the two ingredients.

For each shape use a single pipe cleaner and bend it to form a connected loop, see illustration. You can try any enclosed shape you want, but a flat loop (like a heart or flower petal) is a must. Try to leave a bit of pipe cleaner as a stem to hold onto as you work. You can add a second pipe cleaner to the stem of the first to make it longer, but the actual shape should be made from only a single length of pipe cleaner.

Hold the stem and dip the shape into the glue and coloring mixture. Be sure it is completely immersed, pull it out, and hold it over the bowl until the dripping stops. A colorful film will form inside the bent shape. Should the film pop, dip the shape again, and very carefully and slowly lift it out of the glue mixture. Lay the shape on its edge to dry, or prop it up by sticking the stem into a scrap of plastic foam. If the glue mixture becomes too thick, add a *few* drops of water and stir. The shapes will dry and be ready to do with as you wish in about an hour.

SWEET SMELLER

SWEET SMELLER
(POMANDER BALL)

Sweet smells make us smile. They trigger the imagination and give us nice thoughts and fantasies. It is no wonder, then, that sweet smells attract and excite kids.

A pomander ball is an easily made SWEET SMELLER that gives off its perfume for a long time. Make SWEET SMELLERS for yourself or as gifts to place in drawers, hang in closets, on bedposts, or anywhere you want to have sweet thoughts.

MATERIALS

fruit—oranges, apples,
　lemons or limes
toothpicks
whole cloves
cheesecloth
powdered cinnamon
string or ribbon

TOOLS

scissors

WHAT TO DO

Select a piece of fruit that is ripe, firm, and unbruised. With a toothpick, punch holes all over the fruit. Press one clove into each hole until the fruit is completely covered. If you're very young, you will probably find it easier to punch holes in an apple than in the tough skin of an orange or lemon.

Cut the cheesecloth into a square large enough to wrap the fruit completely. (Nylon netting or any loose-weave cloth that permits the scent to escape will also do.) Place the studded fruit onto the cheesecloth and gener-ously sprinkle powdered cinnamon over it. Enclose the fruit in the cheesecloth, and tie a string or ribbon around the cloth ends. Hang the ball where it cannot be disturbed or bruised for a few weeks until it dries out. As the fruit dries, it shrinks and becomes lighter—the sweet smell will develop and grows stronger. Now it is ready to hang in your room or to give as a present.

Pomander balls keep their fragrance for a long time. If the sweet smell does become weak, sprinkle the ball lightly with water and the smell will return.

SALT GARDEN

SALT GARDEN

If vegetables grow in a vegetable garden, and flowers grow in a flower garden, what grows in a salt garden? Salt, of course! But how do you "grow" salt? Here's how.

MATERIALS

porous stones or coal
salt
warm water
vinegar

TOOLS

cereal bowl
spoon
tablespoon

WHAT YOU DO

Collect a few porous stones or pieces of coal. Porous stones are usually a bit lighter in weight than other stones of the same size, and some appear to have thousands of small holes in them. You may have to experiment to learn what types of stones are the most porous.

Fill the bowl about half-way with water. Start adding salt to the water, one spoonful at a time, and stir until it dissolves completely. You can

"feel" with the stirring spoon when all the salt crystals have melted. Continue to add salt until no more will dissolve in the water. Add about a tablespoon of vinegar to the mixture and stir.

Completely fill the bowl of salty water with the stones you have collected, and put it aside. In less than a day, salt crystals will begin to "grow" on the tops of the stones, creating an

interesting SALT GARDEN. (The salt crystals grow on the stone because they are porous and the salty water can flow up into them. When the salty water reaches the top of a stone, the water evaporates into the air, leaving the salt crystals behind. The vinegar added to the salt water helps "clean" the stones so that the water can flow more easily.) Let the salt crystals continue to grow for several days until all the water in the bowl has evaporated. You can then remove the salt crystal stones or leave them in the SALT GARDEN.

SQUEEZE
PAINTING

SQUEEZE PAINTING

A SQUEEZE PAINTING is made by "drawing" on a plastic bag enclosing some colorful liquid. It's like having a never-ending supply of drawing pads, or a small colored blackboard you draw on with your fingers instead of chalk. The only disadvantage—but not with kids—is that any drawing done with SQUEEZE PAINTING is temporary. It must be erased to start the next composition. You can't make detailed drawings with SQUEEZE PAINTING, but that doesn't matter so much—the fun is really in squeezing and squishing the color in the SQUEEZE PAINTING bag.

SQUEEZE PAINTING is especially good for kids who shy away from drawing because they feel they must compete with better "artists." Even vague, unreal-looking SQUEEZE PAINTINGS are a good exercise to encourage a kid's confidence to do paper and crayon drawings later. If a grown-up wants to show a kid how to draw, he should draw as the child would. If a kid thinks an adult's drawing is better than his, he might be discouraged from trying his own hand.

MATERIALS

clear plastic bag (zip-lock bags work best, but any sandwich or small storage bag will do)
fingerpaint or ketchup or mustard
tape

CONSTRUCTION

Put a few tablespoons of fingerpaint (or ketchup or mustard) inside the bag. Gently squeeze most of the air from the bag and zip-close the top, or close the bag with tape. Smooth the paint evenly with your fingers until it completely fills the bag. If there isn't enough paint to give a solid color all through the bag, add more. Now you are ready for your first SQUEEZE PAINTING. "Draw" over the surface of the bag with your fingers or any smooth ended object such as a spoon or stick. Erase any painting by smoothing over the bag with your fingers.

LUNCH (WITHOUT COOKING)

LUNCH (WITHOUT COOKING)

Many kids enjoy just being in the kitchen with all those wonderful pots, pans, and gadgets to play with. But the real fun for kids in the kitchen is helping to cook the food. No matter what age, there is always a cooking job a child can share with a parent or do alone. When kids help in the kitchen they have fun at the same time they learn to follow directions, to measure ingredients, to time the cooking process, to share their creations and, or course, to clean up.

Good cooking requires organization. Kids should wash their hands, read the chosen recipe, and gather all the ingredients and kitchen tools they will need. (If any ingredients are not on hand, a kid should make a note of what is missing and borrow it from a neighbor, or go along on the next trip to the food market. The food market can be fun for the young cook when he or she is doing the shopping.)

Only recipes that can be made quickly are fun for beginning chefs. Kids can become impatient or disinterested if the recipe takes a long time or cannot be eaten immediately. Each step of a recipe should be carefully followed until the "dish" is completed. But the next time the recipe is made a kid should experiment by adding a little of "this" and substituting a bit of "that." A good cook always experiments a little to try to make the recipe taste better. Personal touches will make it the young chef's own recipe.

There is more to cooking than merely preparing the food. Serve the recipes in a pretty way or turn your lunch into a picnic. Somehow picnic food always tastes best. In fact, a picnic can be food eaten anywhere *but* in the kitchen or dining room.

*　　　　　*　　　　　*

Here are three recipes to make a complete lunch—a main course, a beverage, a dessert—and a bonus recipe for a breakfast treat. None requires the use of the stove. There are no guarantees about nutritional value, only a chance to have fun, work with real kitchen tools, learn the rules of the kitchen, and make a lunch that really tastes good.

PICKLE DOGS

Serves one

2 slices American cheese
1 hot dog roll
1 long slice dill pickle
relish (your favorite kind, mustard or ketchup)
You will need a *knife* to cut the pickle, a *spoon* for the relish, and a *napkin*.

Cut each slice of cheese in two and put the cut slices on the inside halves of the hot dog roll. Put the pickle slice between the slices of cheese. Add relish, mustard, ketchup or whatever you like. Fold the roll together and serve with a napkin.

RASPBERRY FUZZ SHAKE

Makes one large or two small glasses

1 small jar raspberry cobbler baby food
(Other flavor shakes can be made from strained peaches, strained applesauce and apricots, or blueberry buckle baby foods)
1¼ cups cold water
1½ tablespoons honey
⅓ cup non-fat dry milk
You will need a *large jar or container with a tight lid* for mixing and shaking. A plastic container with a tight snap lid is safer for shaking than a glass jar. You will also need a *measuring cup,* a *tablespoon* and a *drinking glass.*

Put the raspberry cobbler, cold water, and honey together in the plastic container and fit the lid on tightly. Shake the container until all the ingredients are well mixed. Add the dry milk, put the lid back on tightly, and shake well for about a minute. Pour the shake into a drinking glass and serve.

A small variation is to add a tablespoon of baking soda with the dry milk to make a RASPBERRY FIZZ Shake.

SWEET CEREAL BALLS

Makes six to eight large cookies

½ cup chunky peanut butter
⅓ cup honey
½ cup flaked coconut
2 cups of your favorite cereal
You will need a *mixing bowl,* a *large spoon* for mixing, a *measuring cup,* a *large cereal bowl* and a *plate.*

Put the peanut butter, honey, and coconut into the mixing bowl and mix the ingredients well. Stir in ½ cup of the cereal and put the remaining cereal into the cereal bowl. Scoop out large spoonfuls of the peanut butter mixture and form it into balls with your fingers. Roll the balls around in the bowl of cereal so the cereal covers the balls completely. Serve on a plate.

NUT BUTTER (A Breakfast Treat)

Here's a bonus recipe that's a tasty breakfast spread for toast, crackers, pancakes or muffins. Unless you get up extra early, you had better prepare your NUT BUTTER the day before.
½ cup or more shelled walnuts or pecans
plastic sandwich bags
You will need a *rolling pin,* a *measuring cup* and a *spoon.*

Be sure all the shells are removed from the nuts. Put the nuts in a plastic sandwich bag and seal the opening. If the plastic bag seems thin, put a second or third plastic bag over the first for strength.

Place the bag of nuts on a hard surface, such as a kitchen counter or cutting board. Pound the nuts with the rolling pin until they break into small pieces. Then roll over the nuts with as much pressure as you can. A friend or anyone strong might help you press down very hard with the rolling pin. As you roll the nuts, the nut oil will ooze out and mix with the fine bits of rolled nuts to make the NUT BUTTER. Keep rolling until the NUT BUTTER is as smooth and creamy as you can make it.

For extra creaminess, you can mix a little regular butter with the NUT BUTTER. Spoon the NUT BUTTER out of the plastic bag and refrigerate it in a small covered container until ready to use.

WORK ROOMS, TOOL ROOMS, BASEMENTS, GARAGES

THREE
STICK
STOOL

THREE STICK STOOL

If you ever need a seat but don't have a chair handy, knowing how to make a THREE STICK STOOL can be a very good thing. Maybe you are playing ball on an empty lot and don't want to sit on the damp ground, or want a seat to relax in near the campfire. Well, you can make a THREE STICK STOOL right on the spot in only a few minutes, or you can make it beforehand and carry the folded stool with you. You can even build a slick version of the THREE STICK STOOL to use around the house with wood dowels instead of sticks. The THREE STICK STOOL is a low-to-the-ground seat, but it is quite strong and deceptively comfortable.

MATERIALS

3 fat sticks (see below)
rope

TOOLS

penknife

CONSTRUCTION

There are many kinds of sticks that can be used to build the THREE STICK STOOL

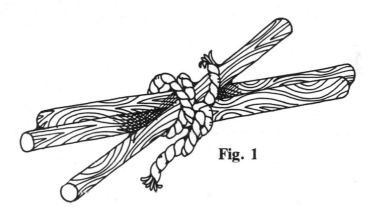

Fig. 1

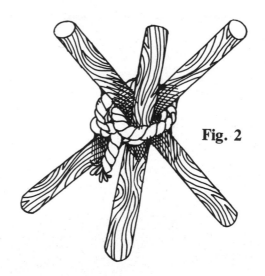

Fig. 2

depending on whether you make it on the spot or in the workshop. Two-inch round fallen branches make good sticks, and so do baseball bats and fat wood dowels. Collect three sticks all about the same thickness and each about three feet long. Exact size is not important. Hold the three sticks together in a bunch and tie a few turns of strong rope very loosely around the center of the bunch, Fig. 1. Be sure that the loop is loose. Knot the rope and cut off the excess. Follow Fig. 2 and spread two of the sticks to form an "X." Spread the third stick to rest in the fork of the other two sticks. Now test the stool. Sit in the "pocket" formed by the three sticks putting each cheek of your bottom on a stick with the third stick at your back. You will find that the stool spreads out a bit and lowers a little, but it is springy and comfortable. Now that you know how to make your own stool, you should never be without a seat.

PADDLE BLOCK BOAT

PADDLE BLOCK BOAT

Most paddle boat construction requires measuring, sawing, and sometimes tedious craftsmanship. But a seaworthy PADDLE BLOCK BOAT can be ready for its maiden voyage in just a few minutes. Whether your "ocean" is the bathtub or a pond, the PADDLE BLOCK BOAT will churn its way

through the water in a quick dash—with a little splash—and then calmly drift to a stop. A PADDLE BLOCK BOAT is only used for short trips. The novelty is that the boat goes "by itself." A kid simply winds the paddle to send his ship off on a fantasy voyage.

Although the PADDLE BLOCK BOAT

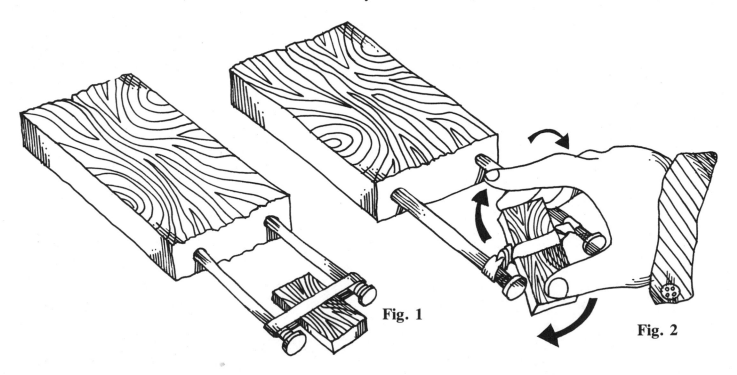

Fig. 1

Fig. 2

cannot carry much real cargo, a few extra wood scraps nailed or glued on, and a touch of art work makes the boat into any kind of ship you want it to be. Every **PADDLE BLOCK BOAT** you make will sail a little bit differently, depending on the size of the wood block, paddle, and rubber band. You might make two **PADDLE BLOCK BOATS** and race them. Remember to wind the paddle to make the boat go forwards. Now, can you figure out what makes the paddle turn, and why the paddle makes the boat go?

MATERIALS

scrap block of wood
thin strip of wood
2 long nails
rubber bands

TOOLS

hammer

CONSTRUCTION

Find a small scrap block of wood. A cut-off from a 2 x 4 is perfect. Hammer the two long nails into one end of the block just far enough so that they won't pull out; keep them as wide apart as possible, Fig 1. Find a fat rubber band that is about as long as the distance between the nails. If the rubber band is too long, double it. If you have only skinny rubber bands, try using two or three together. Stretch the rubber band over the end of the nails. Find a thin scrap of wood for the paddle—one that fits easily between the nails and will protrude beyond their heads. Center the paddle between the rubber band, wind up the paddle, Fig. 2, and you are ready for your first launch.

SIX PACK
HAMMOCK

SIX PACK HAMMOCK

Kids like hammocks better than swings because hammocks are more fun and because their imaginations can invent many different play situations with them. The hammock folds you and as many as two other kids in tight security. A hammock can be a ship loaded with a cargo of branches, leaves, or playthings along with yourself, a tree house, a train, or anything you let it be. You can lean over one of the ends and play ship's lookout. Sometimes a hammock ship is on a stormy sea with huge waves rocking the boat violently. Then there might be a calm with a gently rocking hammock, soothing and restful. Lie back and stare at the sky, or read a book.

Before you decide to build a SIX PACK HAMMOCK, be sure you have a place to hang it. There are no absolute rules about distances between hanging points or height off the ground. If you are going to make your own hammock, it can be constructed to fit the space you have. The most popular place to hang a hammock is outdoors in the shade between two trees. You can also use a single tree in combination with a strong anchoring place like a house or a large post sunk into the ground. If you look hard enough, you will most always find a sturdy hanging point. To hang the hammock, use large screw eyes at the attaching points and mount them about five or six feet above the ground.

Screw eyes can be put directly into a tree without harming it. The actual height of the hammock is easily adjusted, but you still might want to have a helper and yourself hold the hammock in position to be sure your hanging points are properly placed.

Hanging a hammock indoors can be a bit of a problem unless you see two obvious support points such as lolly columns in the basement or beams in the ceiling. You can attach a hammock diagonally between two inside corner walls by attaching screw eyes into the studs through the plaster. Always check to be sure your anchoring points are strong. Don't trust window and door frames. They are usually only decorative moldings and are not strong enough to hold the weight. Most hardware stores carry the screw eyes, hooks, and rings necessary to hang a hammock. Once you have decided on a good hanging spot, you are ready for the construction.

MATERIALS

at least 75 plastic six-pack carriers
clothesline
2 wood sticks
2 metal rings
2 "S"-hooks

TOOLS

scissors
saw
drill and 5/16-inch bit

CONSTRUCTION

First determine the size of the hammock you are going to make. If you have selected a place to hang the hammock, measure the distance between the two hanging points. The "body" or people part of the hammock should be about half that dimension. The harness that supports the hammock at either end will take up the rest of the length.

A good two- or three-kid size hammock (as shown in the photograph) can be made from ninety six-pack carriers—nine across and ten long. You can collect the six-pack carriers over a period of time or you might go scavenging around a campground or a ball park. If you are really in a hurry, a local soda or beer "bottler" who uses six-pack carriers might help you.

The body of the hammock and the harness are both made at the same time by weaving clothesline through the holes in the plastic carriers. The hammock is woven one lengthwise row at a time. Lay out a single row of carriers to the length of the hammock body you want. Place the carriers lengthwise so that their end "circles" interweave and partially overlap, Fig. 1. Now add a second row so that the adjacent circles of the two rows interweave and partially overlap.

Cut a length of clothesline cord a few feet longer than the entire length of the hammock (body and harness). Weave the clothesline the length of the row through the holes in the carrier where they overlap. Weave the cord over, through, under, up, over, through, under up, Fig. 2. Adjust the clothesline so that there are equal lengths of cord at either end.

Continue to add rows of carriers in the same way until the hammock is the width you want. After the last row, weave another length of clothesline through the circles along each of the two outside edge rows.

Lay the hammock flat and square on the floor. To make the "spreaders"—the devices used to keep the ropes separate from one another—find two flat sticks and cut each of them a few inches longer than the width of the hammock. Place one of the sticks at each end of the hammock body and mark the positions of the ropes on the stick. Drill a hole at each mark down the center of the sticks. The holes should be large enough for the rope to go through easily.

Carefully make a single loop knot on each cord where it leaves the body of the hammock. Do this on both sides of the hammock. Place a spreader at each end of the hammock and thread the ropes in order through the holes in the spreaders.

Push the spreaders up against the knots. Using two more lengths of clothesline cord, weave the end circles of the carriers to the spreader sticks. Tie the cord at each end of the stick, Fig. 3.

Gather the cords at one end of the hammock and bring them together at the end. Tie each cord individually to a large ring, being sure to adjust each cord so that the hammock will lie flat on the floor with no cords kinking. Snip off any excess cord ends.

You can hang the hammock directly to the support eye hooks using "S"-hooks, or using two more "S"-hooks and two short lengths of chain, you can make the hammock height adjustable.

The SIX PACK HAMMOCK requires no maintenance and can be used outdoors year round. It is strong and safe for adults as well as kids.

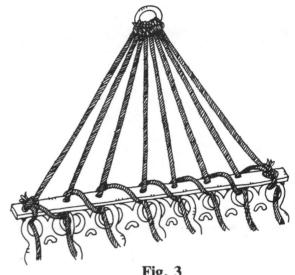

Fig. 3

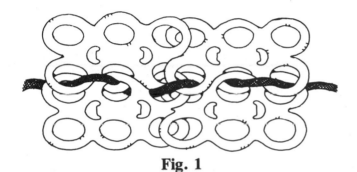

Fig. 1

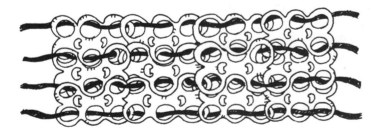

Fig. 2

KIND ANIMAL TRAP

KIND ANIMAL TRAP

The first animal trap was probably a large balanced rock that fell on the creature when it touched the bait and sprung the trap. Since then, people have invented all kinds of traps to trick animals into being caught. Although there will always be "better traps" invented, most animal traps kill or injure their prey. The KIND ANIMAL TRAP is one more "better" trap, but this one catches the creature unharmed. The small animal is attracted to the bait inside a coffee can, but as the animal goes inside, a mechanism is triggered that slams shut the can lid trapping the animal unharmed.

Depending on the area of the country where you live, there are many small animals that can be caught in the KIND ANIMAL TRAP just to look at: lizards, mice, moles, chipmunks, turtles, frogs, woodchucks, and many other woodland creatures. Be careful! All animals become scared when caught, and a few can be vicious or carry disease. Know the animals that live in your region and whether there might be any danger from them. Observe the caught animal in the trap and then let him go in the same area in which he was trapped. Wear gloves if you intend to handle the animal. If you want to keep the animal for a short time, you will have to learn about the animal's natural habitat and what it eats, then build it a suitable cage. The KIND ANIMAL TRAP is not large or comfortable enough to be used as a cage.

Most important, do remember that you have left a set trap, and check it every few hours. At first you will probably want to check the trap every few minutes. But an animal must first be attracted by the bait and then venture into the trap. Don't be discouraged if there is no action right away—but don't forget to keep checking the trap. If left in the trap too long, an animal without food and the proper environment could die.

MATERIALS

coffee can (1, 2 or 3 lb. size) with
  a plastic snap-on lid
mouse trap
plastic drinking straw
¼ x 1-inch bolt and nut

TOOLS

drill and ¼-inch bit
pliers
screwdriver or wrench (to fit the bolt)
fat nail
scissors

CONSTRUCTION

To build a KIND ANIMAL TRAP you must first start with an unkind animal trap—a mouse trap. Remove and discard the "bait clip" from the trap by pulling out the staple that holds it in place. Put the plastic lid firmly on the open can top. Put the can on its side. Pull back the spring-loaded arm on the mouse trap and, sliding the "free" end of the trap beneath the can, allow the spring-loaded arm to close against the lid, Fig. 1. Hold the mouse trap firmly in place on the can, and drill a one-quarter-inch hole through the mouse trap and the can. Put the bolt through the mouse trap into the can, then open the can by bending down the plastic lid, reach in and put a nut on the bolt. You may need someone to help you hold the can while drilling and fastening the nut.

Tighten the bolt and nut securely. Push the can lid and the spring-loaded arm down flat against the mouse trap and see where the lid touches the fastener holding the "trigger arm." Cut or punch a hole in the lid with a fat nail at that point, then let the lid back up enough to slip the trigger arm through the hole in the lid. Push the lid down against the mouse trap again. Cut a piece of plastic drinking straw about two or three inches long, and slip it over the trigger arm. To set the trap, hold the lid down and slide the straw on the trigger arm so that its end catches on the protruding screw threads of the bolt, Fig. 2. Be careful, it takes a delicate hand to set the trap.

Most animals eat just about anything that people eat. Put the bait inside the can, then set the trap out where it can be easily checked.

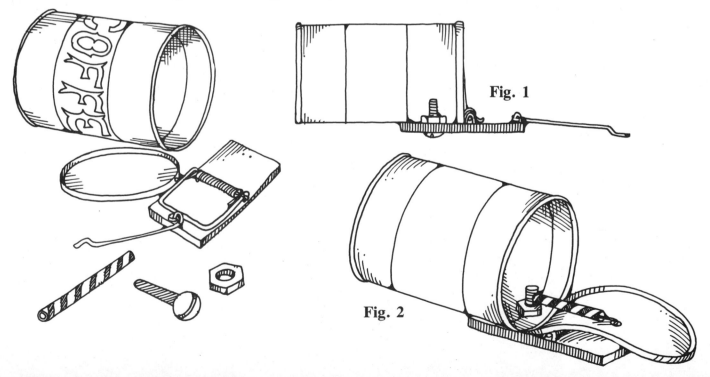

Fig. 1

Fig. 2

TUBE DOME

TUBE DOME:
a one-frequency 3/4-sphere icosahedron dome

Dome building has become increasingly popular in recent years. All types of domes have been built, from simple playground climbers to structures meant to be lived in. People are beginning to discover that the dome is quite a remarkable phenomenon. Domes, the strongest and lightest building system ever invented, use the least amount of materials to enclose a space; there are no posts needed inside a dome to hold up the roof. Domes are easy to build from simple materials, they are pretty to look at, and children instinctively want to get in or climb onto them. Inside a dome, no one can be in a corner.

But domes are not a new invention. People have been building and living in domes for thousands of years. Igloos, mud huts, wigwams, and yurts are all traditional kinds of dome houses. What *is* new are modern ways to build domes. In the 1950's a technology was developed to build domes by putting triangular sections together. This system is called "geodesic" dome building. The completed

TUBE DOME shape is called a ¾-sphere icosahedron. A full icosahedron has twenty faces and as a structure would have five more struts on the bottom than the ¾-sphere shape—an impractical form for a dome. "One-frequency" means that all the struts are the same length. The dome might sound complicated but it is not. By joining twenty-five equal length struts (each forty-two inches long) you will get a kid-sized, all-weather dome that will measure about six feet across and four and one-half feet high. What you call the dome after it is built is your choice. By covering the dome with a blanket or sheet, it can be a playhouse or a fort; if you cover the dome with a clear plastic (polyethylene) drop cloth, it can be a mini-greenhouse; and with a simple variation to make the struts stronger, the dome can be used as a climber.

Before you start to build a TUBE DOME, it is best to build a dome model first. It will be easier that way to understand dome principles and the construction process involved. It is also interesting to play with the concept of scale—you will see the relationships between the model and finished structure, and the ways in which alterations in scale proportions will affect the size of the finished structure. An easy way to construct dome models is by using the STRAW AND CLIP BUILDING method described on page 68.

While building the dome model, you might try a simple experiment to understand why geodesic domes are built from triangular sections and not squares or rectangles. Connect four straws to form a square. Holding opposite corners of the square, try to shift it and change its shape. You will find that it is pretty easy to do. Now remove one of the straws and connect the remaining three to form a triangle. You will find that the triangle is very rigid and cannot easily be twisted out of shape. The triangle is a rigid structural building unit, and domes built from triangular sections are strong and rigid.

MATERIALS

100-foot roll of ½-inch black PVC tubing (see below)
25 ½ x 36-inch wood dowels
11 3/16 x 2-inch round head bolts with nuts
22 flat washers to fit the bolts

TOOLS

hacksaw
propane torch
clamping vise
¼-inch bit and drill
measuring tape
screwdriver

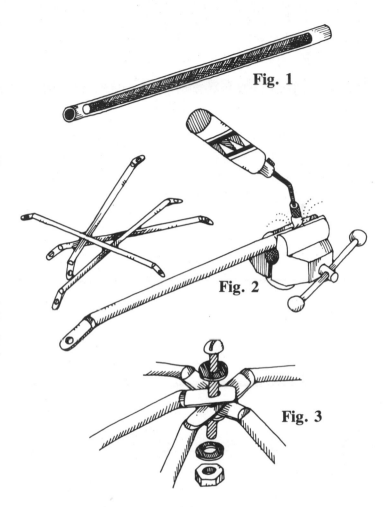

Fig. 1

Fig. 2

Fig. 3

CONSTRUCTION

To build a TUBE DOME requires a few "complicated" workshop tools and should be done by an adult with children assisting.

The size of a dome is limited only by its design and the length and strength of the building struts you use. The TUBE DOME has been designed to use inexpensive ½-inch PVC tubing and ½-inch wood dowels. The plastic tubing is available at most hardware or plumbing stores and comes in 100-foot rolls. That is enough tubing for one dome with a little to spare. Although the tubing is called ½ inch it actually measures about ¾-inch round with a 9/16-inch hole. The ½ x 36-inch wood dowels are exactly that size, and are available at most hardware or lumber stores.

If you intend to build a dome for climbing, you will have to use larger "¾" or "1-inch" plastic tubing with wood dowels or thin wall electrical conduit that will fit inside the tubing.

All twenty-five struts of the TUBE DOME are the same length and made exactly the same way. Measure and cut twenty-five pieces of tubing each forty-two inches long. Place a 36-inch dowel in each tube centered between the tube ends, Fig. 1. Crimp flat a few inches of both ends of each tube in a vise. The tube ends will stay flat if they are heated with a propane torch either just before or while in the vise. Keep the torch flame moving, and don't concentrate it in any one spot or the tubing could melt and burn. Drill a one-quarter-inch hole through each flattened tube end about one inch

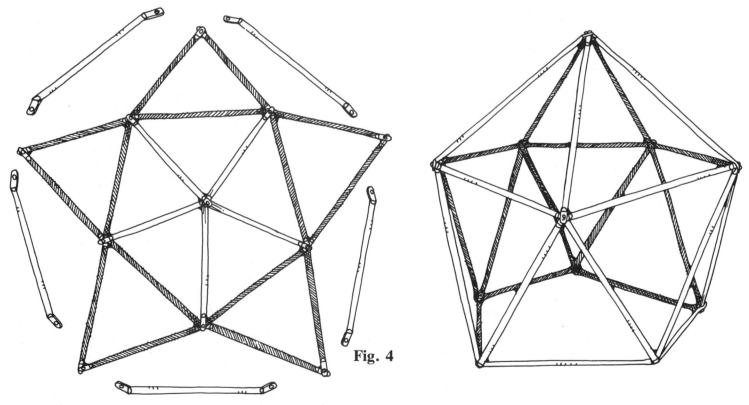

Fig. 4

in from the tip, Fig. 2. Now that the struts are completed the dome can be assembled.

Start by connecting one end of five struts together using a bolt, two washers, and a nut. Spread the five struts out in a star pattern, Fig. 3, and then lay out the remaining twenty struts as shown in Fig. 4. Using the same bolt, nut, and washers assembly, attach the struts in the pattern shown. To attach the five base struts you will have to lift the structure and the dome will then take its shape.

All the bolts should point in the same direction. If the dome is to be permanently covered, have the bolts point outward so that the covering can be attached to them. Otherwise, have the bolts point inward.

The base of the completed TUBE DOME might be a bit wobbly unless the bottom struts are anchored to the ground. That's because the dome is not a complete icosahedron.

If you are excited about dome building there are many good books that explain how to make domes of all types and sizes.

MUSICAL NAILS

MUSICAL NAILS

Almost anything will make a musical sound if you know how to play it. Playing a homemade instrument can sometimes be more fun than playing the "real thing." No talent or lessons are necessary to play MUSICAL NAILS. You bang out sweet sounds, or try to figure out a simple tune. Even if you want to, you cannot make bad music.

MUSICAL NAILS can be a good introduction to making music. Sometimes, however, it's difficult for a kid to try a musical instrument for the first time. In that case, a parent might encourage a child to bang on MUSICAL NAILS along with a familiar record or song on the radio. The joy of recognizing a tune may be all the "inspiration" needed. A child should never be forced to play music, though. Before he can play, he must like to listen. Young kids would rather sample musical instruments than be serious about them. A parent should explain how an instrument works, but not insist that a kid play real music. A child's imagination will turn the sounds he makes into his own "real music." Of course, a child may show no interest in MUSICAL NAILS whatsoever. All is not lost. The NAILS may be hung outdoors as a lovely wind chime.

MATERIALS

different-sized large nails
thin strong string (nylon sewing thread is good)

CONSTRUCTION

If you cannot find a variety of large nails in your home or at a nearby building site, buy an assortment of nails at the hardware or building supply store. Try to have at least six or eight different sizes. Tie a length of string to each nail head. (The string should be thin and strong; if is too fat, it will make the MUSICAL NAILS sound dull.)

Find a place to hang the MUSICAL NAILS—from a railing, rung or back of a chair, coat hanger or table edge.

You will need a "banger" to "play" the nails. Another large nail is good, or you might try other objects, like a stick or spoon, to hear the different sounds they make.

HOW TO PLAY

Pick up the longest or fattest nail by its string

and strike it with the banger. It should make the lowest tone of all the nails. Do the same with the other large nails, and hear if any of them makes a lower sound. Test all the nails, then hang them in order from the lowest tone (on the left) to the highest tone (on the right). Now strike each nail from left to right. Do you hear a good DO, RE, MI, FA, SOL, LA, TI, DO? Probably not! Nails were never meant to play musical notes. But that's okay, you can still try to play songs you know or invent your own.

For those who want to perfect the art of MUSICAL NAILS, there is a way the nails can be tuned to exact pitch. You can raise the pitch of a nail (make a higher tone) by cutting or filing off some of its length. If you spend enough time filing and testing, you can make a good musical-nail xylophone.

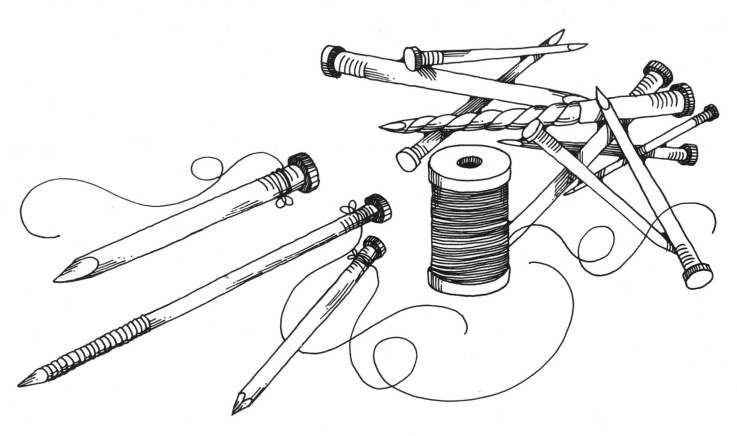

GAME STICK

GAME STICK

A deck of playing cards or a checker board with markers do not become games until someone adds the rules. Change the rules and you have a brand-new game. With a checker board and checkers you can play American, English, French, and Polish checkers, Diagonal checkers, Cops and Robbers, and many other games that use a sixty-four-square game board and markers. Of course there are hundreds of card games you can play.

The GAME STICK may also be played many different ways depending on the rules used. You can play solitaire games, or competitive games with another player. Three sets of game rules for the GAME STICK are described here—Piles of Two, Switching Sides, and Not the Last One—but after learning these games you should have little trouble inventing your own. Part of the fun is seeing whether your own game rules really work.

MATERIALS

wood stick about 1 foot long
1- to 2-inch finish nails (nails without heads)
25 to 40 plain washers

TOOLS

saw
hammer
ruler
pencil

CONSTRUCTION

Place the stick down on one of its wider sides and measure out ten equally spaced "positions" along the top. Be sure to leave some "margin" between the end positions and the ends of the stick. Use ten finish nails all the same size, and hammer a nail just as far as it takes to hold it firm at each position mark down the center of the stick. Place twenty-five to forty plain washers over the nails depending on the game you will play (the washers should not overlap each other), and the GAME STICK is complete. (To keep the washers from being lost between games, put all the washers on the nails and stretch a long rubber band over the nails from one end to the other.)

You can make a fancier version of the GAME STICK if you like. Cut, sand, and

stain a wood block for the base and use pieces of dowel instead of nails; drill holes in the block and glue the dowels into them. Red rubber garden hose washers can be used over the wood pegs as marker pieces.

HOW TO PLAY

All games played on the GAME STICK require moving the washers (or markers) from one peg to another in order to solve or win the game. All ten pegs, or only a few, are used depending on the game rules as well as the number of washers placed on a peg. Other rules deal with the type of moves allowed, for example, "forward moves only," "jumps only" or "no two markers on any one peg." Here are three games with rules to get you started.

Piles of Two is a simple puzzle solitaire game. Put one washer on each of the ten pegs. You can only move by jumping any washer or marker over two other consecutive markers. The object is to make five adjoining piles of two markers. Now try to do it in only five moves!

Switching Sides is another solitaire puzzle, but this game can be very tricky. Mark three washers with a crayon or felt marker so they can easily be distinguished from the plain washers. You might also use three washers of a different size or color. Use only seven of the ten pegs, and starting from one end of the GAME STICK, put a single marked washer on each of the first three pegs. Skip one peg and put a single plain washer on the next three pegs. The object of the game is to reverse the positions of the washers so that the three marked washers occupy the spaces of the three plain washers and vice versa. However, you must play by these rules. You can move a marker one peg or jump it over an adjoining marker only. Only one marker can occupy a peg. Markers cannot move backwards. It may seem impossible, but it can be done. Now play the same game using four markers to a side.

Not the Last One is a competitive game for two players that involves either a bit of strategy or a lot of luck. Use only four consecutive pegs, and place between six and ten washers on each of the pegs. All four pegs should have the same number of washers. Each of the two players in turn must remove as many washers from a single peg as he chooses. He can remove one, two, three... or the entire pile. (As players remove washers they can be stored on an unused peg.) The object is *not* to be the player who must take the last washer.

KNITTING
FRAME

KNITTING FRAME

Another version of the WEAVING SPOOL (page 193) is the KNITTING FRAME, but instead of weaving cords, the KNITTING FRAME produces a woven yarn mat that can be used to make other projects such as wall hangings, quilts, purses or whatever you like. There are three variables to the KNITTING FRAME that will determine the size and texture of the weaving. The wider the slot in the frame, and the further apart the nail spacing, the looser the weaving will be. The length of the frame determines the width of the weaving, and the yarn you select determines the texture. You might try making several looms, each with different spacings, to find the weave that you like best.

MATERIALS

scrap strips of wood (see below)
carpet tacks or short nails
yarn
toothpicks, nail, or pencil

TOOLS

saw
hammer

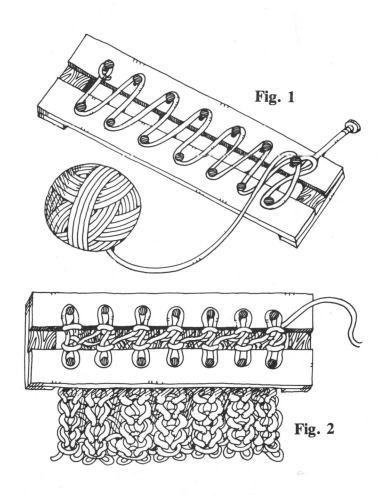

Fig. 1

Fig. 2

135

CONSTRUCTION

Find two strips of wood a bit longer than the width of the weaving you want to make, or cut one long strip in half. Position the two strips so that they are parallel and about an inch or two apart. Cut two smaller strips of wood the length of the distance between the long strips to brace them, and nail them at each end of the long strips, Fig. 1. Use carpet tacks or short nails (no flat heads) about an inch long, and hammer them about an inch apart into one of the long wood strips. The nails should be hammered in about halfway. Nail another row in exactly the same way and opposite the first row, on the other long strip, Fig. 2.

HOW TO WEAVE

Place the KNITTING FRAME in front of you and knot the yarn around the nail in the upper left corner. Weave the yarn down and around the nail below it and then up and around the second top nail. Continue winding the yarn around the nails in this same way to the other end of the frame. When you have reached the last nail, wind the yarn back, one nail at a time, following exactly the same pattern.

As you wrap the yarn around each post, lift the bottom loop up and over the top loop and the nail. As you weave back and forth across the KNITTING FRAME, the woven piece will slip through the opening in the middle of the frame. To finish off the knitting, weave the end of the yarn alternately from one side of the frame to the other through each of the loops on the posts. Remove the weaving from the frame, pull the yarn end snug, and knot.

ROLL
BACK CAN

ROLL BACK CAN

The ROLL BACK CAN might seem a mystery even though you've built it yourself. If you give the ROLL BACK CAN a push, it will roll across the floor, slow down and stop, hesitate a moment, then roll all the way back to you. Actually, there is nothing mysterious if you understand what happens inside the can as it rolls. When you push it, the plastic can lids rotate and wind up the rubber bands against the weight in the center, which does not turn. The more the can rolls, the more the rubber bands will wind, building up "unwinding" energy. When the can stops, the built-up energy unwinds the rubber bands which send the can back to you. See how far you can roll the can and still have it come all the way back. The record distance so far is twenty-eight feet!

MATERIALS

large, round tin can (a 1- or 2-pound coffee can or large fruit juice can work well)
2 snap-on plastic lids that fit the can
rubber bands
heavy weights (fishing sinkers, bolts or nuts)

TOOLS

fat nail

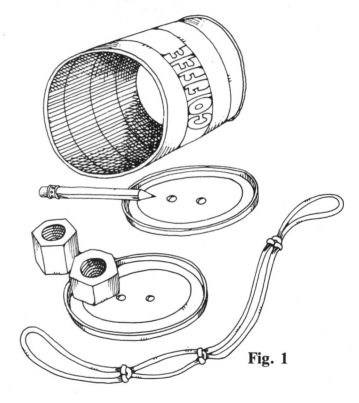

Fig. 1

can opener
stubby pencil or twig

CONSTRUCTION

Remove both the top and the bottom of the

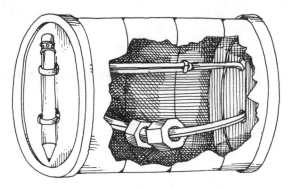

Fig. 2

can. Be careful. The metal lids you remove are sharp, and they should be discarded immediately in a safe place. Using the fat nail, punch two holes in each plastic lid. The holes should be equally distant from the center of the lid and at least one inch apart, see Fig. 1. Connect a sufficient number of rubber bands together so that their total length is about twice the length of the can, but no longer. (The type of rubber bands you use will affect how well the ROLL BACK CAN works. If the rubber bands are too skinny, they may not wind up enough energy to send the can back. If the rubber bands are too fat, they will not wind up

enough, and the ROLL BACK CAN will only travel for a short distance. Experiment for best results. Feed the ends of the connected rubber bands through the holes on the outside of one of the plastic lids. Put that lid on the can so that both ends of the rubber band strand are inside the can. Slip the weight onto only one end of the strand, and then put the ends of the rubber bands through the inside holes of the other plastic lid, Fig. 2. You might have to stretch the rubber bands a bit. Connect a short pencil or a twig through the two rubber band loops on the outside of the bottom lid, and then snap the lid on the can.

Test the ROLL BACK CAN by giving it a small push on the floor. If the weights continuously scrape against the can, then the rubber bands are too loose or the weights are too heavy. Experiment and make whatever corrections are necessary. To work well, the ROLL BACK CAN should be used on a smooth floor. The can just does not work well on carpets or other rough surfaces. Here's a little trick to help you get the greatest travel. Pre-wind the rubber band to take up slack by rolling the can a few feet in the direction you will send it, then give the can its push.

THE WAVE MACHINE

THE WAVE MACHINE

Danger! The liquids necessary to make THE WAVE MACHINE are dangerous if not handled and used properly. Therefore, this project should be done *only* with an adult to supervise. But don't let the danger warning discourage you from building THE WAVE MACHINE. The magnificent, slow-motion waves that will roll through this "ocean in a bottle" are just too good to miss. Scientists have made giant wave machines to study the very complex motions of waves. Your waves won't be as large or as scientifically correct as those made by a scientist, but the graceful rolling and crashing blue "water" inside the bottle is guaranteed to be impressive. Now you don't have to be satisfied just holding a conch shell to your ear to hear the roaring ocean. You can see it in a bottle!

MATERIALS

large transparent soft plastic bottle (dishwashing detergent or household cleaner bottle, for example) with a screw top that fits tightly.
rubbing alcohol
blue food coloring
paint thinner

CONSTRUCTION

Make sure not to use a glass bottle—the possibility of broken glass is too risky. Remove any labels from the bottle, and rinse it out

thoroughly. Fill the bottle about one-third full with rubbing alcohol. Add the blue food coloring, a drop at a time, and gently shake the bottle until the alcohol is a nice "ocean blue"! Fill the bottle the rest of the way to the top with paint thinner. Tightly screw on the bottle cap. There should be no air at all inside the bottle.

MAKING WAVES

Hold THE WAVE MACHINE on its side with both hands and gently rock the bottle back and forth to create the waves. You will soon develop the best rhythm for making gentle sea rolls or foamy crashing waves—all in slow motion. The secret of THE WAVE MACHINE is that the alcohol and the paint thinner do not mix together (the food coloring mixes with the alcohol). Sometimes after a lot of rough use the liquids in the bottle become quite cloudy. Put THE WAVE MACHINE aside for a few hours, and the liquids will become clear again.

JACOB'S
LADDER

JACOB'S LADDER

Almost a century ago JACOB'S LADDER was a novel toy that parents would buy to amuse their children. The toy is still fun today, but the only way to have one now is to make it yourself. JACOB'S LADDER is made by connecting a chain of thin wooden blocks with cotton tape in such a way that the toy will give the illusion, when worked, of the wood blocks tumbling over each other and down the "ladder." The toy is sometimes known by other names such as "clacker blocks," because of the rhythmic slapping sound the blocks make while "falling." However, the original name is JACOB'S LADDER, which comes from the Bible, Genesis 28-12. In this passage, Jacob dreams of a ladder stretching from earth to heaven on which angels make their way ascending or descending.

MATERIALS

thin wood strip (if you need to buy wood, a
    three-inch wide plank of bass wood balsa
    from the hobby store is perfect)
½-inch twill tape

TOOLS

wood saw

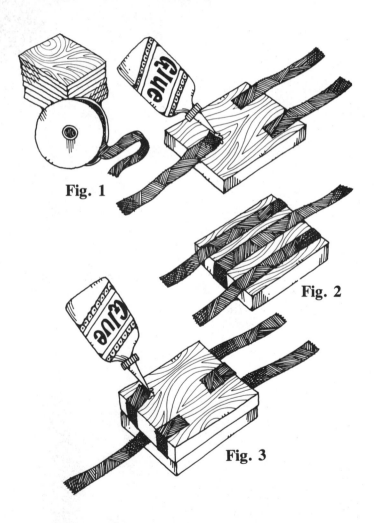

Fig. 1

Fig. 2

Fig. 3

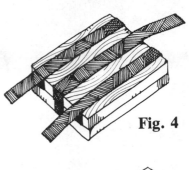

Fig. 4

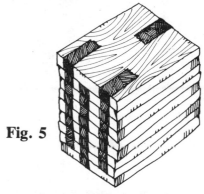

Fig. 5

sandpaper
glue

CONSTRUCTION

Make at least six, or as many as ten, wood blocks about one-quarter-inch thick each. The block size isn't important, but all the blocks must be exactly the same size. After cutting the blocks, sandpaper all the edges until they are smooth. At this point you might want to paint the blocks, but it is not necessary. Cut the cotton twill tape into many pieces, each about twice as long as one of the wood blocks. Glue three pieces of tape to all but one block, as shown in Fig. 1. When the glue has dried, turn all the blocks over. Take one of the blocks and fold the three tapes up and across the plain face of the block, Fig. 2. Place a second "taped" block on top of the first, tapes down, then fold the three short protruding tape ends from the first block up and over onto the top face of the second block, and glue the tape ends in place, Fig. 3. Now take the three long tapes protruding from between the blocks and fold them up and across the face as you did to the first block, Fig. 4. Continue to add blocks in this way, ending with the one plain block, Fig. 5. When completed, the blocks will fold like an accordion into a neat pile.

THE ILLUSION

To work the JACOB'S LADDER illusion, hold either end block by the edges with the other blocks hanging free below. Tip the end block as if you were going to touch it flat against the next block down. Now tip the block over to its other side. This will start the tumbling action. Continue tipping the top block back and forth, and the toy will show a mysterious rippling action that appears as if the blocks were all tumbling down the ladder.

TIRE TREAD
SHOES

TIRE TREAD SHOES

So much of what we throw away has a possible second use if only you can think of what it might be. Before you throw anything away, see if there are any parts of it that can be salvaged for future projects—nuts and bolts, cloth, hardware, or wire, for example. If the discard is primarily made from one material—like a car tire or a soft plastic wastepaper basket—think of the properties of that material and what project could use them. Discovering what a material can do will often suggest new uses for it. Will it bend or hinge on itself, can it easily be cut, will it weather outdoors, can you fasten it to other materials and how, does it require a protective finish, will it float? Sometimes you can reverse the process by first deciding what to make and then listing the properities that materials for your project will require. Now ask yourself which discards have those properties.

If you were going to make a pair of shoes from scrap discards, what materials would you look for? The soles would have to wear well, be comfortable, flexible, and waterproof, yet not slippery. The sole material must also be strong enough to protect your feet from pebbles, rough surfaces, or pointed things you might step on. Can you think of a discard material that has all these properties? Tire treads! By cutting the tread and adding a bit of strapping cut from an

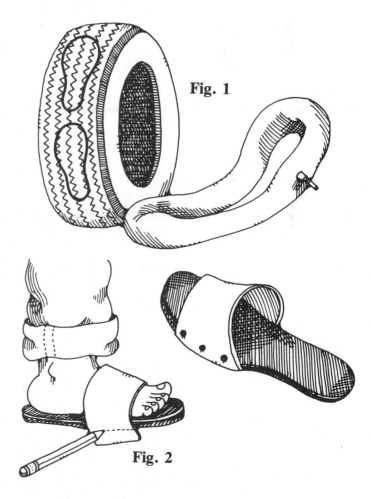

Fig. 1

Fig. 2

inner tube, you can make a pair of TIRE TREAD SHOES.

MATERIALS

worn-out car tire (see below)
old inner tube
carpet tacks

TOOLS

drawing chalk or soap
matt knife or fine-tooth saber saw
scissors
hammer

CONSTRUCTION

Visit your local gas station or tire dealer and ask for an old worn-out tire and tube—they are usually free. With a piece of chalk or a chip of soap as a marker, trace the outline of both your right and left shoes on the tire tread, Fig. 1. Cut out the two sole patterns using a matt knife or a fine-tooth saber saw. You must be careful, tire rubber is tough to cut. If you use a matt knife, point the blade to the side away from yourself. With scissors, cut two strips of inner tube rubber about three or four inches wide. Now put your bare or socked foot on one of the tire tread soles, tread side down, and wrap one inner tube strip across your toes. Remember that there is both a right and left sole. Mark a line on either side of the strip even with the bottom of the sole, Fig. 2. Cut the rubber strip on the lines, and fasten it to the edges of the sole with carpet tacks and a hammer. Do the same thing with the tire tread sole for your other foot. Your new pair of TIRE TREAD SHOES are ready to wear.

There are many other styles of TIRE TREAD SHOES you can make using the tire tread sole and some type of strapping. To get ideas, look in magazines and newspapers for shoe advertisements showing interesting designs.

BACKYARDS, PORCHES, PICNICS, EMPTY LOTS

COLLECTIONS

COLLECTIONS

nails
autographs
buttons
shells
insects
coins
bells
advertising buttons
menus
rocks
pencils
grave stone rubbings
screws
nuts and bolts
beads
bottle caps
baggage labels
stamps
sugar packets
postcards
dolls
miniature cars
drinking straw wrappers

newspaper clippings
corks
postmarks
maps
marbles
butterflies
posters
old radio tubes
fingerprints
fabric swatches
playing cards
matchcovers (without matches)
bottles
leaves
knots
photographs
greeting cards
buckles
keys
flowers
cash register slips

Kids are natural collectors of almost anything, but to have a COLLECTION means that you try to save as much of a particular thing as possible. Look at the suggestions above and see if there is something to collect that really interests you. These are only suggestions. You may have your own ideas, but be sure that what you choose to accumulate is pretty much available. (It would be difficult to start a sea shell collection if you lived in Iowa.) Once you've chosen something to collect, start by gathering all of it you can. If you and a friend decide to collect the same thing, you can help each other and swap-off duplicates. After a while, most collectors will specialize in one aspect of their collection. A postcard collector may decide to specialize in cards with pictures of statues or bridges. A button collector may try to find only metal or wooden buttons.

To enjoy your COLLECTION and show it off to others, you should have a way to store and display the pieces. A notebook is good for flat collections, such as stamps, postcards, leaves, and matchcovers. Tape each piece of your collection in place and make a few notes on the page telling where you found the piece, and the date. Collections of larger objects can be stored in boxes. An egg carton is good for buttons, keys or marbles, and a shoe box lined with cotton makes a good display for shells, rocks or pencils.

If you become serious about collecting, there are clubs and magazines for almost every kind of collector. You might ask your library for books and magazine articles about your particular kind of collection. Collecting can give you the chance to be a young authority on a certain subject, and you might someday wish to call yourself a numismatist (coin collector), or even a philatelist (stamp collector). You'll feel quite proud.

PLAY
BOOMERANGS

PLAY BOOMERANGS

Real boomerangs cannot be considered a toy. In fact, native hunters of Australia use boomerangs as hunting weapons with great skill and accuracy. When thrown properly, the boomerang will spin through the air in an arc that will return it to the thrower—and that's the fun. The boomerang is actually a small flying machine that the thrower controls by his skill. PLAY BOOMERANGS are small cardboard versions of the hunter's weapon that really work, yet they are safe enough to fly indoors. There are many easy-to-make boomerang shapes that will fly, but the performance of any boomerang depends on the skill of the thrower. It usually takes some practice before you can make the PLAY BOOMERANG return to your feet consistently.

MATERIALS

thin cardboard scrap (back of a paper tablet, shirt cardboard, pieces from a shoe box, etc.)

TOOLS

pencil
ruler
scissors

CONSTRUCTION

The illustration shows four designs for PLAY BOOMERANGS that will fly easily. Try them all to see which one flys best for you. How well a particular boomerang flies depends on the cardboard you use and the "flying skill" you develop. Copy one of the boomerang designs onto a piece of cardboard. The illustrations are full-sized, and it would be best if you copied the design exactly. Later, you might experiment with increasing or reducing the size of a boomerang to see what effect it might have. Carefully cut out the design with scissors and you are ready for your first test flight.

THROWING

Depending on size, cardboard thickness, and the design you have chosen, each PLAY BOOMERANG will have its own flight characteristics. The boomerang might fly in a large arc, go straight out and then come straight back. Some will fly in a small circle just a few feet in front of you. You will have to practice and experiment.

There are two methods for putting a PLAY BOOMERANG into flight. The easiest way is to hold your hand at eye level. Rest the boomerang on the back of your hand with one leg of the boomerang reaching out over your hand. Then using the pointer finger of your other hand, strike the leg of the boomerang sharply.

The other method of throwing is a bit more difficult, but will often give a better flight. Hold the middle of the PLAY BOOMERANG *very lightly* between your thumb and index finger at eye level so that two legs point to you. Then with the pointing finger of your other hand, sharply strike the leg. Whichever method you find works best, you will have to practice to get the feel of it before all your boomerang flights find their way back to you.

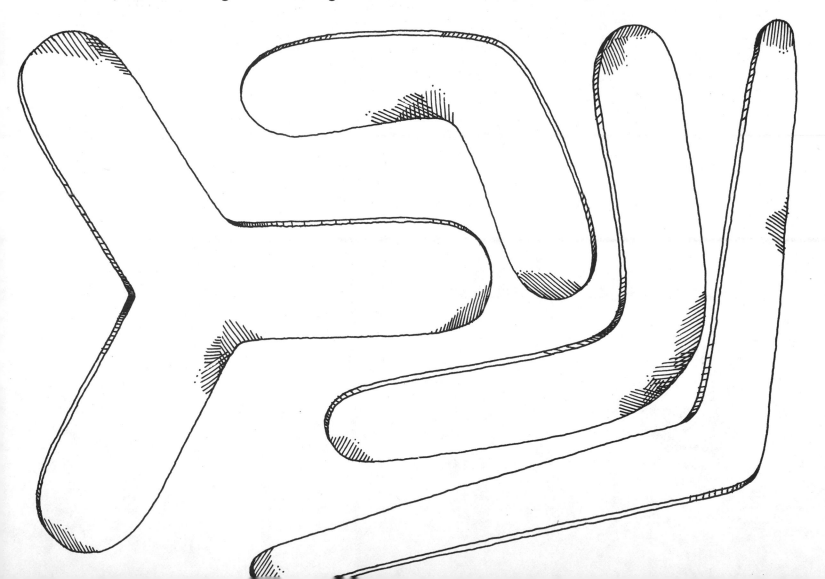

BOTTLE GARDEN

BOTTLE GARDEN

A BOTTLE GARDEN is a small but very efficient terrarium for growing plants indoors away from their natural environment. Even if the growing conditions where you live are terrible—pollution, dry air, or poor soil—many types of plants will grow successfully in the high humidity of a BOTTLE GARDEN. A flourishing BOTTLE GARDEN not only provides a close-up view of nature, but can also be an interesting decorative piece.

There are three conditions necessary for maintaining a BOTTLE GARDEN—moisture, temperature, and light. The closer you come to meeting the conditions of the native plants, the more lush your BOTTLE GARDEN will grow.

Because the BOTTLE GARDEN is completely sealed, moisture cannot escape and the plants need to be checked for moisture only occasionally. If the plants or leaves show signs of wilting, you will know that it is time to add a little water. Temperature is very important. Most BOTTLE GARDEN plants grow best at room temperature or warmer. Keep the BOTTLE GARDEN in a warm room where the temperature is reasonably constant. All plants require light-energy to survive, but don't "cook" the plants in direct sunlight. A window sill with shaded sunlight on the south side of your house is perfect.

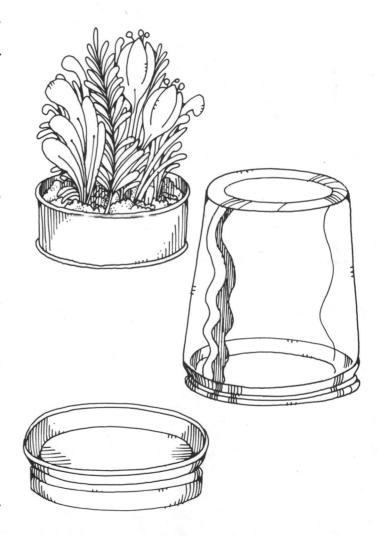

159

Unless you sow seeds, what you plant in the BOTTLE GARDEN depends mostly on the native plants available in the region where you live. Find a damp shady spot in a nearby wood or park, and gently dig up plants and seedlings small enough to fit in the BOTTLE GARDEN. Keep the plants moist and wrapped in a plastic bag until you replant them. Some common plants that grow quite well in a BOTTLE GARDEN are ferns, moss, wildflowers, grasses, small seedling of trees, and many other small woodland plants.

MATERIALS

tunafish-sized tin can
large untinted open-mouth bottle or jar with a screw lid (giant-sized peanut butter jar,
   for example) which will fit over the tin can
gravel or small pebbles

TOOLS

hammer and fat nail
garden hand spade

CONSTRUCTION

Completely remove the lid from a tunafish-sized tin can. Using a hammer and a fat nail, poke three or four holes in the bottom of the can. Put a quarter-inch or so of gravel in the bottom of the can, then fill it the rest of the way with soil from the ground where you have gathered your plants. Moisten the soil by sprinkling it with water, but don't make the soil muddy. Carefully transplant the varieties you have gathered by poking a hole in the soil with your finger, and inserting the plant roots into it (with the dirt ball that surrounds the roots if possible). Arrange the plants so that the shorter ones are nearer the edge of the can.

Remove any labels from the bottle and wash it thoroughly. Place the tin can on the inside of the jar lid, and then lift the lid and can up into the jar and screw the lid closed. Your terrarium is completed.

Newly transplanted plants usually need a few days to become accustomed to their new environment. After you have found the correct balance of moisture, temperature, and light, your BOTTLE GARDEN will grow and flourish with only a minimal amount of attention.

SOLAR
HEATER

SOLAR HEATER (AND HAND WARMER)

During the winter, when the sun doesn't provide enough heat to keep us warm, we usually burn some kind of fuel in a furnace to create our own heat. The typical fuels we use are wood, coal, gas, and oil. The greatest source of fuel and heat, however, is still our sun, and many people are now experimenting with and inventing better ways to collect the sun's energy to heat houses and run machinery.

One device already used to collect the sun's energy is a "solar furnace." The solar furnace is usually a disk-shaped mirror aimed at the sun. The curved mirror acts as a lens which focuses a large area of the sun's rays into a smaller area. The smaller area becomes much hotter than the air around it because it is actually receiving more sunlight.

You may have already experimented with the

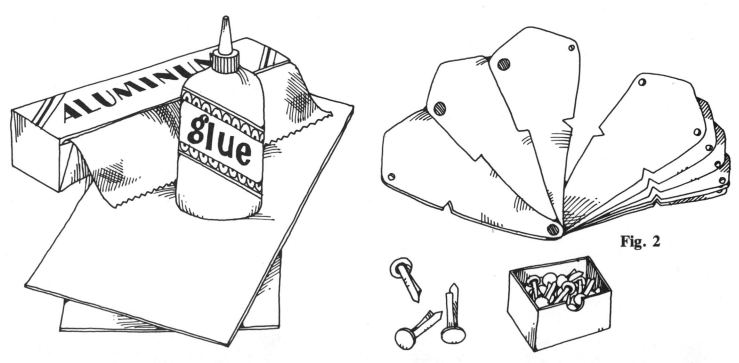

Fig. 2

sun's energy by holding a small magnifying lens in sunlight to set fire to a leaf or a scrap of paper. Some campers use a lens and the sun to start their campfires. But be very careful... The concentrated sunlight can become very hot. Some large solar furnaces can create enough heat to melt almost anything on earth.

You can build a small solar furnace that won't become hot enough to hurt you but will keep your hands toasty warm on a cold day. The solar heater is constructed by attaching pieces of foil-covered cardboard together to form a disk shape. When the SOLAR HEATER is aimed directly at the sun, it will concentrate its heat in an area a few inches out from the center of the disk. Aim the SOLAR HEATER at the sun and prop it up against a rock or tree to warm your hands or for doing experiments. (As the earth turns, the position of the sun in the sky changes, so every fifteen minutes or so re-aim the SOLAR HEATER to collect the most sunlight and create the most heat.) If you are scientifically minded, you might try putting a thermometer in the SOLAR HEATER'S center and compare that temperature to the ambient (surrounding) air temperature outside. Whether you build a SOLAR HEATER as a practical hand warmer or as a science experiment, you are learning how to use an energy source that is free and will almost never run out—the sun.

MATERIALS

scrap cardboard—shirt boards, shoe and gift
   boxes, heavy file folders, etc.
aluminum foil

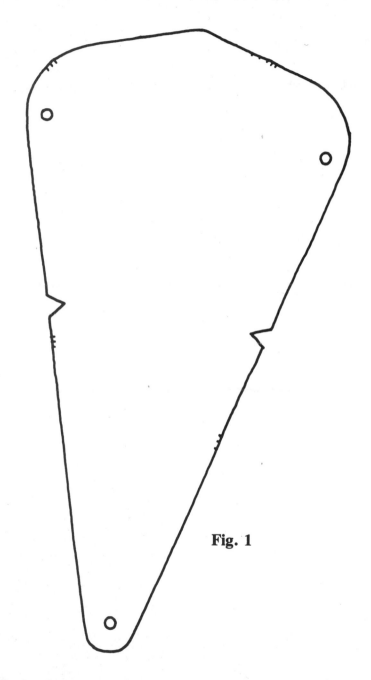

Fig. 1

liquid white glue, mucilage, glue stick or
   spray glue
tracing paper
paper fasteners

TOOLS

pencil
scissors
hole punch

CONSTRUCTION

The SOLAR HEATER is made by fastening ten foil-covered leaves of cardboard together to make a disk-shaped reflector. Find ten scrap pieces of cardboard of about the same thickness. Glue a piece of aluminum foil—shiny side up—to each cardboard piece. Try to keep the foil flat and free of wrinkles, but it is not important that it be mirror smooth. Trace the leaf shape, Fig. 1, *exactly*, and then retrace the shape onto the ten pieces of the foil-covered cardboard. Be sure to mark the position of the three leaf holes on each piece of cardboard. Carefully cut out all the leaves, and punch the holes with a paper punch or the point of a pencil.

Stack the leaves in a pile with the foil sides up, and place a paper fastener through all ten leaves at the narrow base. Bend over the two paper fastener legs. Follow Fig. 2, and attach the leaves in order, starting with the top leaf. Interconnect the notches at the sides of the leaves, and attach the top adjoining holes with paper fasteners. You should have to bend any two adjoining leaves to line up the top holes. It is this bending that creates the disk shape. When you have connected all ten leaves together, your SOLAR HEATER is ready for testing. See if you can get more heat by removing one of the leaves to get a deeper disk shape. By removing all but the center paper fastener, the SOLAR HEATER can be folded to a convenient size for carrying.

SUN
CLOCK

SUN CLOCK

Before mechanical clocks or watches were invented, and for the last two thousand years, sundials were used for telling time. Some sundials were gigantic, the size of buildings, and some were so small they could be worn as a ring. Although we have more accurate and reliable clocks today, the sundial is still one of the simplest time tellers ever invented. All you had to do was read the position of the shadow on the sundial face to tell what time it was. If the shadow was halfway between four and five o'clock, then the time was about four thirty. The only problem, of course, was a cloudy day or nighttime when there were no sun shadows.

There are many types of sundials, and most of them have to be calculated and constructed mathematically for a particular placement on earth. For example, a sundial that has been made to tell time accurately in Florida will not tell correct time in Maine. The SUN CLOCK is a version of an "equatorial sundial" and is the only type of sundial that will tell accurate time anywhere on earth. However, an equatorial sundail must be positioned so that it is parallel to the earth's equator, and requires a small adjustment depending on where in the world you live.

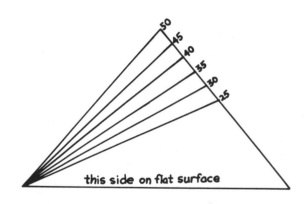

this side on flat surface

MATERIALS

large clear or semi-transparent plastic can lid
new pencil

TOOLS

ballpoint pen or laundry marker

CONSTRUCTION

The plastic can lid will be used to make the face of the SUN CLOCK and must be layied out accurately with hour markings. If you have a protractor and can do simple geometry, lay out the can lid in twenty-four equal, spaced radial lines from the center (15° segments). If you don't know how to do it that way, you can use a less accurate but satisfactory method. Draw a line completely across the top face of the lid through the center. (Most soft plastic can lids are made of a slippery plastic that is best written on with a ballpoint pen.) Draw a second line across the lid face through the center perpendicular to the first line. Now the lid is divided into four equal parts. Draw two more lines through the center, dividing each quarter in half. The lid is now divided into eight equal parts. Using your best judgment, divide each of the eight spaces into three smaller equal spaces by drawing two lines from the center to the edge in each space. You should have twenty-four equally spaced radial lines emanating from the center. If the SUN CLOCK could work all day and night, each one of the radial lines would represent one hour of the day. But no sundial can work during the night, so you only need to mark those hours when there is usually some daylight. Use the ballpoint pen or a laundry marker to write the hours at the edge of the radial lines. Start with any radial line and mark it 5, then going clockwise mark the next radial 6, then 7 and so forth up to 12. After 12, start at 1 and number through 9. If it stays light outside past nine P.M. where you live, continue to mark the radials with whatever additional hours you need.

Using a new full-length pencil with a point, poke the pencil through the exact center of the lid, top to bottom. Push the pencil through about halfway. The pencil serves two functions: it casts the shadow that gives the time and it acts as a stand to support the SUN CLOCK.

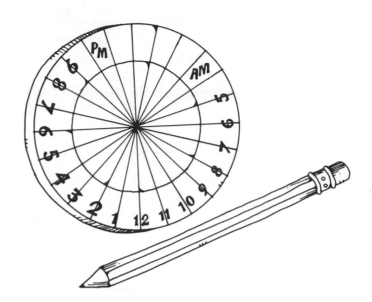

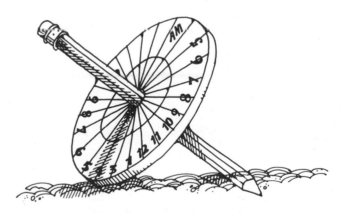

The eraser end of the pencil acts as the "gnomon" or the part that casts the shadow, the pointed end of the pencil supports the SUN CLOCK and is meant to be stuck in the ground so that the SUN CLOCK will keep its position and not be blown away.

Look for a good sunny spot outdoors at which to station your SUN CLOCK. If that is inconvenient, you can always place it on a sunny windowsill inside, but you will only be able to read the SUN CLOCK during the hours when the window is sunny. If your indoor or outdoor sunny spot is not a place into which you can stick the pencil, try using a flowerpot filled with earth.

Before you stick the pencil stand into the ground, you must set it at the proper angle for where you live. Ask someone or find out what the latitude of your city is. Latitude is a measurement of distance from the equator that is marked on most maps. You don't have to be precisely accurate—within 10° will do. Here are some typical latitudes. If you live near any of these cities, use that latitude to adjust your SUN CLOCK.

Phoenix, Arizona: 35°
Los Angeles, California: 35°
San Francisco, California: 35°
Miami, Florida: 25°
Atlanta, Georgia: 35°
Chicago, Illinois: 40°
Portland, Maine: 45°
Boston, Massachusetts: 40°
Minneapolis, Minnesota: 45°
New York, New York: 40°
Houston, Texas: 30°
Seattle, Washington: 45°

Once you have determined your approximate latitude, make a tracing of the angle most closely corresponding to your latitude, from the angle chart. Using this triangular piece of paper as a gauge, push the pencil into the soil at the angle which corresponds to it. If you are placing the SUN CLOCK directly into the ground or some other fixed spot, have the eraser-tipped gnomon end of the pencil pointing directly north. If you are mounting it on a flowerpot, you can turn the flowerpot so that the gnomon points north.

Push the pencil into the earth at least a few inches so it is firmly anchored, then slide down the SUN CLOCK face until its bottom edge rests on the ground. Rotate the SUN CLOCK face until twelve o'clock is directly at the bottom.

If the sun is out, check the SUN CLOCK to see if it reads the correct time. Use your watch or a clock in the house. You may have to make adjustments for small construction errors, north direction, or daylight saving time. Rotate the face slightly, or reposition the pencil until the SUN CLOCK reads the correct time. From then on the SUN CLOCK should give you the accurate time.

Between March 21 and September 23 (spring and summer) the shadow of the gnomon will fall on the top face of the SUN CLOCK. From September 23 to March 21 (fall and winter), the shadow will be created by the underneath support end of the gnomon and will fall on the underside of the SUN CLOCK face. But because the face is either clear or translucent plastic, you will be able to see the shadow and read the time correctly on the top face.

LAZY FISHING

LAZY FISHING

Going fishing can be a marvelous thrill for a kid, especially for the first time, but too often his expectations are greater than the actual experience. Young kids have a very hard time just sitting and waiting. If the fish do not seem to be biting, a child will get squirmy and bored. He will want to pull the line in every few minutes to see if "just maybe" a fish has been caught. When that activity yields little results, the child will often resort to the fun play he already knows—playing with the water, mud, and stones. Often it is best if a kid's first fishing experience is planned around some other family outing—a boat ride, swimming, or a picnic. Then the child will not center all his expectations for fun around just one activity.

Learning to fish is a gradual process. Fishing with sophisticated equipment can be frustrating at the beginning. There are too many things to learn and to do right. Even if a parent is an experienced fisherman, he would do well not to expect a child to understand or learn everything shown him. When a child catches his first fish, it will inspire confidence and he will then be ready to be taught some finer points. The important thing, always, is to have fun.

One way to avoid the anxieties and expectations of a first fishing trip is to go LAZY FISHING. LAZY FISHING lets you go

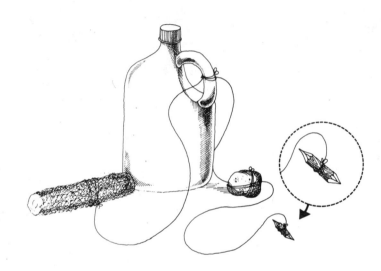

through all the preparations of setting up the rigging, baiting the hook, and dropping the line. But then the LAZY FISHING set-up will take care of itself, and a kid can go off to do something else. It will be more exciting for the child to check back once in a while to see if a fish has been hooked.

CONSTRUCTION

THE HOOK
One of the most common fishing accidents is being stuck with a sharp hook. Before a kid is

taught to use a regular fishing hook, a "gorge hook" will do. Simply whittle down both ends of a small hardwood twig, and tie the fishing line to the center. The gorge hook should be baited only on one of the pointed ends. When the fish swallows the bait with the hook and then swims away, the hook will twist crosswise in the fish's mouth and hold firmly.

THE SINKER

Any small rock can be used as a sinker. You might need to experiment to determine how heavy a rock you need, but start with a rock about the size of a ping pong ball. Attach the fishing line to the sinker a foot or so above the hook by wrapping the line securely around the rock several times, and tying a knot.

THE FLOAT

This is the secret of LAZY FISHING. Instead of using the customary "bobber," the float is made from a large empty plastic jug with the cap tightly fitted. The fishing line is attached to the jug handle so that the bait will hang a few feet above the water bottom. You may have to guess just how long the line should be. When a fish bites and is hooked, it will not be able to pull the jug below the water and the tension on the fishing line will keep the hook secure in the fish's mouth. When a fish is caught, you will see the jug swishing and bobbing, and that's the signal to haul in the line.

FISHING LINE

Here it's best to use the "real thing!" Common string is just not strong enough for fishing and will not do. Don't buy a fancy fishing line, just one reel of strong, inexpensive fishing cord. The line should be wound around something that will float—just in case! A fat stick or a corn cob will do nicely.

BAIT

All fishermen have their favorite baits and you will probably come to favor a specific bait yourself. Any of the following baits can be used for LAZY FISHING, depending on availability.
worms
crawfish
small toads
minnows
crickets
grasshoppers
dough balls (flour mixed with water)
A good job for kids preparing to go fishing is to be in charge of getting the bait. (That's something kids are best at.)

When it's time to go fishing, just throw the whole LAZY FISHING apparatus into a stream, lake, etc. You can take off now if you wish, but remember to check back from time to time to see if the jug is bobbing. You don't want to let that big one get away.

PAPER BAG BLOCKS

PAPER BAG BLOCKS

Building with small blocks can accommodate play fantasies with dolls and toy cars, but building with big blocks can accommodate *you*! Large, lightweight PAPER BAG BLOCKS and other large-scale blocks encourage active play and imaginative building. A simple block or a whole block construction is anything a kid's imagination wants it to be. The constructions can be settings for other types of play, or they can be knocked down immediately to begin another and different structure. Parents should not be concerned about the destruction of a laboriously built "castle." Often a kid wants to assert himself and control his environment. It is the process of building that's most important.

Once an environment is built, safe materials may be added to it to aid in the play drama. Young builders can supplement the block constructions with pieces of old cardboard boxes to make ramps, roofs, and bridges.

If PAPER BAG BLOCKS get too damp or water-soaked they should be left in the sun or brought inside to dry. The blocks may be used indoors as well as out.

MATERIALS

large grocery bags
old newspapers
tape (preferably masking or package-sealing
tape)

CONSTRUCTION

Lay a grocery bag flat on a table. Fold the top over a few inches, and crease the bag on the fold. Open the bag completely, and stuff it with ten to twelve double-page sheets of crumpled newspaper. Fold the bag on the crease lines and tape the top closed. There is no need to paint or decorate the blocks—unless you want to.

Make at least ten PAPER BAG BLOCKS—or more if you have bags and storage. Try using different-sized bags for smaller or larger blocks.

173

WATER SLIDE

WATER SLIDE

How can you keep cool on a warm summer day when the beach is far away and you can't find a friend with a pool? A grassy backyard with a WATER SLIDE is how. Water is always a good play friend, and the WATER SLIDE is great for active play—sliding, splashing, running. Any number of kids can play. Put on your bathing suit and get in line. When it is your turn, take a few running steps and flop yourself down on the slippery, wet plastic sheet. Try side slides, belly flops, sitting slides, head-first or feet-first slides. If you get a good start, you will slide the entire length of the plastic sheet and onto the grass!

MATERIALS

large plastic sheet (an inexpensive
   dropcloth)
2 big stones, scrap board, or other weights

TOOLS

water hose
lawn sprinkler

CONSTRUCTION

Do not build a WATER SLIDE on any hard surface. Grassy ground is soft and safe for active play. Spread the plastic sheet over the grass smoothly. Hold the top end of the plastic down with any weight, such as big stones or a scrap (splinter-free) board. Place a lawn sprinkler along the side of the plastic sheet and turn on the water so the spray falls on the plastic. When the plastic is completely wet, you are ready to start your slides. Keep the sprinkler on for as long as you play.

One warning! Every half hour move the plastic sheet to an alternate location so that the grass underneath will not get "cooked" by the sun.

YO-YO, BOLO AND BOUNCERS

YO-YO, BOLO AND BOUNCERS

The word YO-YO is strictly American, but the toy was enjoyed more than three thousand years ago by Roman and Greek children. Since then, YO-YOs of all kinds have been made by people all over the world. In most societies, YO-YOs were made as simple amusements, but in the Philippines the YO-YO was also used as a weapon to skillfully zonk an enemy in the head. Some toys using string and balls or weights have also been given the name YO-YO—like the French *Bandelure*, or "Eskimo Yo-Yo," which is actually Bolo.

The following instructions show you how to make three types of YO-YOs: THE BUTTON YO-YO, which is a small version of the tradition yo-yo; BOLO, in which you try to get two balls on the ends of a string to orbit around in opposite directions; and BOUNCERS, a simpler version of BOLO for younger players.

BUTTON YO-YO

MATERIALS

4 large buttons

string

TOOLS

scissors
needle and thread

CONSTRUCTION

Find four large buttons all the same size. The larger the buttons, the better the YO-YO will work. Nest the buttons together in pairs, and then put the two pairs back-to-back so that the curved sides face each other. Align the holes in all four buttons, and using a needle and thread sew them together tightly. Cut a piece of string about two to three feet long. Tie one end of the string around the center between the button pairs, snipping off the short end of string from the knot. Test your BUTTON YO-YO to decide exactly how long the string should be. Cut the string a little beyond that length, and tie a loop at the end to fit your finger.

If you don't already know how to work a

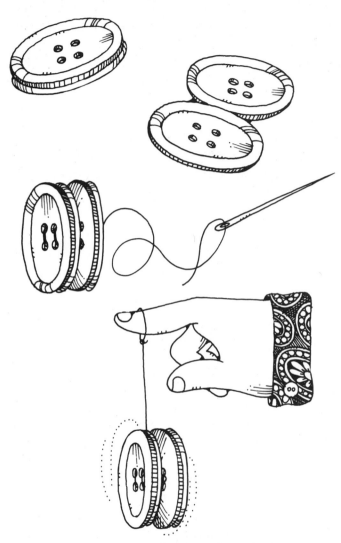

the string, then start to climb back up the string. But unless you give the YO-YO some help, it won't make it all the way back up. The trick is to give the string a slight jerk up just *before* the YO-YO reaches the bottom of the string. Practice until you can keep the BUTTON YO-YO going up and down continuously.

BOLO

MATERIALS

2 rubber balls, about the size of golf balls
heavy twine

TOOLS

scissors
medium-sized nail

CONSTRUCTION

Use a medium-sized nail to poke a hole through the center of one ball and out the other side. Cut a piece of twine about three-feet long. Double up the twine at one end a few inches, and using the nail poke the doubled twine through the hole in the ball and out the other end. Tie a knot or two in the looped piece of twine protruding from the ball, then pull on the long end of the string to be sure that the knot will keep the twine from slipping back through. Now attach the second ball to the other end of the twine in the same way.

The object of BOLO is to get both balls

YO-YO, here are instructions to get you started. Wind the string around and around in the groove between the buttons. Put the string loop on your pointer or middle finger and hold the YO-YO between that finger and your thumb. Let the YO-YO go. As the YO-YO falls, it will unwind until it reaches the end of

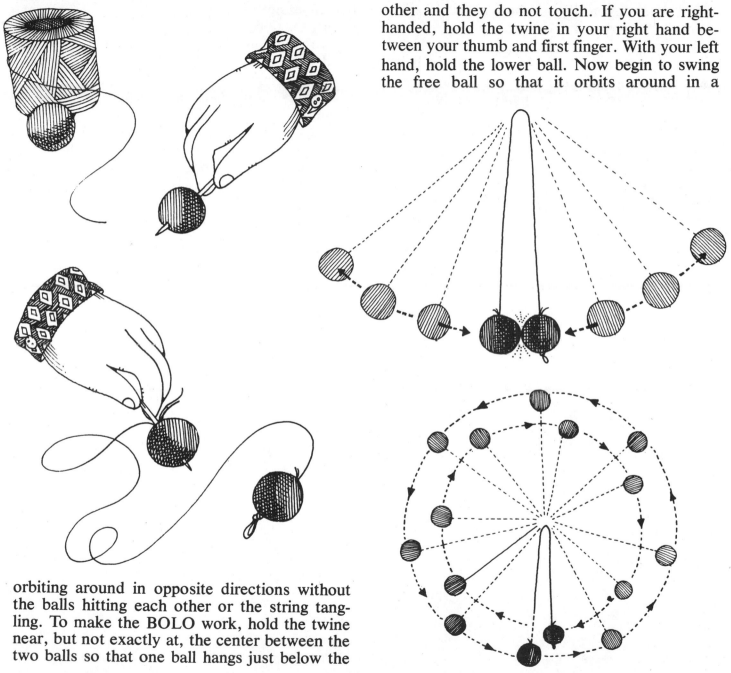

other and they do not touch. If you are right-handed, hold the twine in your right hand between your thumb and first finger. With your left hand, hold the lower ball. Now begin to swing the free ball so that it orbits around in a

orbiting around in opposite directions without the balls hitting each other or the string tangling. To make the BOLO work, hold the twine near, but not exactly at, the center between the two balls so that one ball hangs just below the

179

clockwise circle (from your point of view). When you have that ball going well, start the other ball orbiting in a counterclockwise direction with your left hand. To keep both balls orbiting, you will have to practice to learn the rhythm of jerking your hand slightly up and down at just the right time. Once you get it, you will be able to do it every time, so challenge a friend and watch him struggle.

BOUNCERS

For those kids who have difficulty mastering BOLO, BOUNCERS is just as exciting, but much easier to do. The object is to keep the two BOLO balls bouncing against each other in an arc without "missing." Construct the balls and twine exactly as for BOLO. Hold the twine in the center using your thumb and first finger. The balls should hang so that they are even. (It is helpful to some kids if a knot is tied at the exact middle of the string to show where the string should be held.) With your free hand, lift one ball up to the side, and let it go. As the ball falls back and strikes the other ball, jerk the twine up slightly. Practice until you get the proper rhythm to keep the balls bouncing. Now count how many bounces you can go without missing.

FROG JUMPERS

FROG JUMPERS

Although most kids enjoy the activity of organizing tools and materials before doing a project, there are some toys to be made and enjoyed right on the spot—without preparation. If a kid "learns" a project by doing it a few times, just recognizing the needed materials will often suggest that "something to do." FROG JUMPERS is not a major time-absorbing activity, but it is a fun project that a kid will often initiate himself. With a friend, FROG JUMPERS can become a game to see whose "frog" can jump the highest, the farthest, or over some obstacle. (As with any action toy, a kid should remember to keep FROG JUMPERS away from his eyes.)

MATERIALS

very thin "Y"-shaped twig from a fallen branch
straight twig
rubber band

CONSTRUCTION

The thinner the "Y"-shaped twig selected, the higher the "frog" will jump. Break off enough of the tops of the "Y" shaped branch to make them a few inches long, and break off the stem of the twig, so that it is easy to hold. A

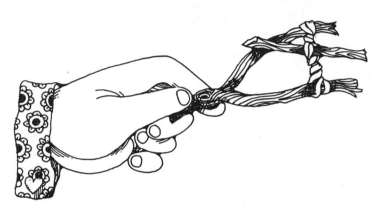

dried wishbone from a chicken or turkey will also do. Stretch a thin rubber band across the tops of the twig, and put a small straight piece of twig through the rubber band, midway between the branches. The straight twig should be short enough to just miss touching the middle of the "Y" twig.

FROG JUMPING

There are two ways to make the frog jump. Wind the straight twig into the rubber band ten or fifteen turns, hold the FROG JUMPERS down on a flat surface, and then move your hand quickly aside. The straight twig will spin around causing the FROG JUMPERS to shoot up in the air. Another way is to wind the small twig, and then turn it slightly sideways so that it stays in place on the side of the "Y" stick. Then put the FROG JUMPER down carefully. With a long stick give the FROG JUMPER a nudge until the twig slips and the frog jumps.

Sometimes FROG JUMPERS jump up, land, and jump up again. It is hard to predict exactly how the frog will jump. Sometimes you have to keep experimenting with different twigs and rubber bands until you have made a champion jumping frog.

WILD BEAST
WHISTLES

WILD BEAST WHISTLES

Wild beasts belong outdoors and so do WILD BEAST WHISTLES. By simply folding a strip of paper in a special way, you can make a whistle that will imitate the loud roars of wild beasts in the jungle. What's nice is that you can make the whistle in a minute almost anywhere—and without tools. But never blow a WILD BEAST WHISTLE, or anything that makes a loud sound, near someone's face. Ears are very sensitive, and they can be hurt by harsh or loud sounds.

WILD BEAST WHISTLES were made many years ago using thin strips of birch bark. At one time, they might have been used by hunters to make "animal calls," or maybe for "secret calls" between friends. But you can decide how you want to use your WILD BEAST WHISTLE yourself (it makes a great "Bronx cheer!").

MATERIALS

thin paper

TOOLS

scissors

CONSTRUCTION

Each WILD BEAST WHISTLE you make will give a slightly different roar. Cut a long strip of thin paper. The length or width of the

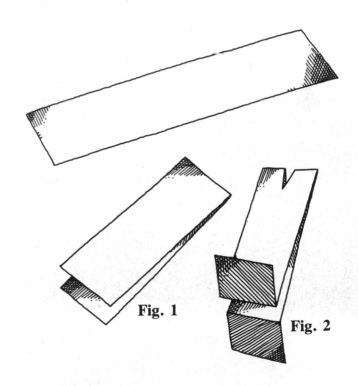

Fig. 1

Fig. 2

paper strip does not seem to make much difference, but thin-paper WILD BEAST WHISTLES make deep sounds and are easy to blow. Heavy paper will make a higher pitched sound, but will be more difficult to blow.

Fold the paper strip in half lengthwise and crease, Fig. 1. Fold one end of the strip up and the other end down and crease, Fig. 2. Now cut or tear a notch in the middle of the folded end, Fig. 2. The notch allows the air you blow to pass through—if it is too small you will have to blow harder. To make the whistle work, hold the WILD BEAST WHISTLE loosely between two fingers close to the folded ends. Put the paper ends up against your lips and blow hard between the folded strip. The air you blow causes the paper to vibrate, making the wild beast roar. It is easy once you get the hang of it, but you might need a little help or practice at first. If you have trouble making the roar, be sure that you are holding the paper loosely. You might also try using a thinner piece of paper, or making the notch a bit larger.

CARS, TRAINS, PLANES, RESTAURANTS

PANTS CARRY BAG

PANTS CARRY BAG

"A place for everything and everything in its place." That's just what you'll have with your own PANTS CARRY BAG to organize and carry stuff like crayons, paper, books, a comb, dolls—even clothes. A kid can use a suitcase or a shopping bag for a trip to the beach or an "overnight" at a friend's house, but the PANTS CARRY BAG is really special—six pockets to pack: two in the front, two in the back, and two made of the legs. Most kids are delighted to pack a bag for a trip (even if it is only going to a neighbor's house) but the PANTS CARRY BAG makes the packing even more fun. If the trip is going to involve travel time, the CARRY BAG may be prepared to carry "play as you go" things and projects such as crayons, paper, books, dolls, Lego, puppets, and a few very personal belongings. A kid always has special things to take with him and he needs something to put them in. The PANTS CARRY BAG really fills the bill.

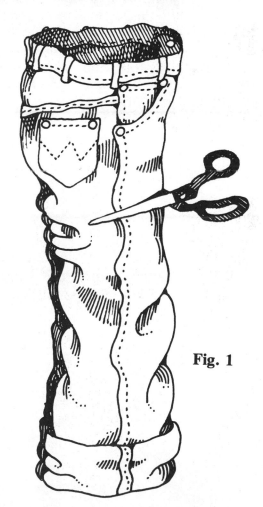

Fig. 1

MATERIALS

old pants saved from the rag pile
rope or an old belt

TOOLS

scissors
needle and thread

CONSTRUCTION

The size of the pants determine the size of the PANTS CARRY BAG. Pants with pockets and a zipper fly front usually give you more compartments. Using large scissors, cut off the pant legs a few inches below the crotch, Fig. 1. (The cut-off pant legs can go to the rag pile.) Fold the pants inside out and with a sewing needle and strong thread, sew straight across the bottom of each cut-off pant leg.

Fold the pants right-side out. You will need a rope or cord for the drawstring and handle. Fancy cords are nice, but a piece of clothesline or even an old belt will work fine. Cut the cord about a foot longer than the waist. Thread the cord through the belt loops, and tie the cord ends together. Crab (pull up) the cord between the loops on either side of the pants to make handles and pull to close the PANTS CARRY BAG, Fig. 2. Depending upon the length of the cord you use, the bag can be hand-carried or slung over your shoulder.

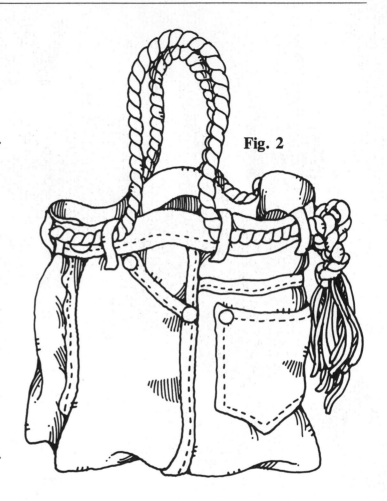

Fig. 2

WEAVING SPOOL

WEAVING SPOOL

Next to using your fingers to weave on, one of the simplest types of looms is the WEAVING SPOOL. Depending on the size of the weaving spool and the yarn or string used, thin or fat cords can be woven and then made into fancy ropes, sashes, belts, spiral rugs or just decorations. But when kids weave, the fun is often not in the finished product, but in the skill it takes to weave yarn into interesting designs.

There are three simple ways to make a WEAVING SPOOL, and each will produce a somewhat different looking cord. A WEAVING SPOOL made from an empty wooden cotton thread spool is best used with string because the hole in the center of the spool is small and can only accommodate a skinny cord. A WEAVING SPOOL made from the top of an empty plastic detergent bottle will produce a loose, open-weave tubular cord. A WEAVING SPOOL constructed from paper cups and large paper clips can be varied in design to make fat, skinny, loose or tightly woven cords.

With all three WEAVING SPOOLS, the yarn or string you use will determine somewhat the character and texture of the weave. The heavier the yarn, the tighter the weave will be. After you have made and woven on a few different WEAVING SPOOLS, you will probably know which spool and yarn combination produces your favorite cords.

THREAD SPOOL LOOM

MATERIALS

large wooden cotton thread spool
push pins

TOOLS

hammer

CONSTRUCTION

Select a large wooden thread spool and ham-

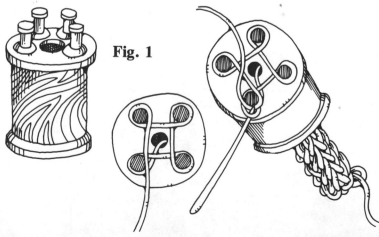

Fig. 1

mer four posts evenly spaced around the hole at one end of the spool. Push pins make excellent posts, Fig. 1. Or you can use short nails or carpet tacks, letting them extend about one-quarter to one-half above the spool.

BOTTLE TOP LOOM

MATERIALS

large round plastic detergent bottle

TOOLS

scissors
pencil

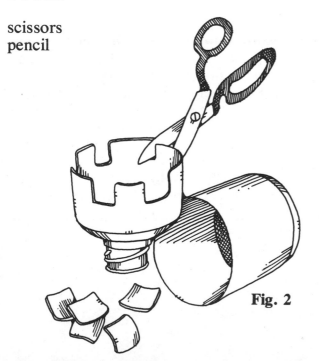

Fig. 2

CONSTRUCTION

Using scissors, cut off the top of a plastic detergent bottle a few inches down from the neck. Throw the bottom away or save it to store your weaving yarn. Draw a pattern of evenly spaced, square-shaped posts around the cut edge of the bottle top. You can make as many posts as you like, but do make at least four. The more posts you make, the tighter the weaving pattern will be. Now cut the plastic away with scissors to form the posts, Fig. 2.

PAPER CUP CLIP LOOM

MATERIALS

3 paper cups of the same size
giant-sized paper clips
glue

CONSTRUCTION

Arrange as many paper clip posts as you like, but at least four, around the top lip of one ot three paper drinking cups. Be sure to use giant-sized paper clips or the posts will be too small, and the yarn will slip off. The paper clips should be attached to the cup so that the two pointed "legs" of each paper clip go over the outside of the cup. Position each paper clip so that about half its length is inside the cup.

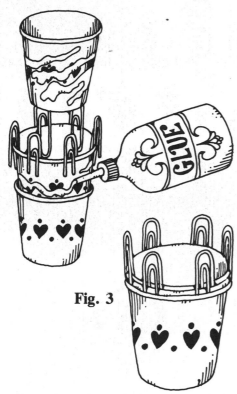

Fig. 3

Apply glue around the outside of the cup and push it firmly down into a second paper cup. Spread glue around the outside of the third paper cup and push it down inside the paper clip cup, Fig. 3. Let the glue dry and then cut a hole about half the diameter of the cups through their bottoms.

HOW TO WEAVE

MATERIALS

yarn or string

TOOLS

round toothpick, skinny nail, or a pointed pencil

There are a few different techniques for weaving on a WEAVING SPOOL that someone might show you. Here is one that will work on the three types of spools that have been described. Follow the illustrations carefully until you have learned the weave.

Select the string or yarn you want to use and drop the end of the yarn down through the hole in the center of the WEAVING SPOOL. Going counterclockwise around the spool, wind the yarn once around each post until you are back where you started, Fig. 1. Now begin again at the post where you started, and wind the yarn as before once around the post above the first loop on the post. Using a thin pointed object like a round toothpick, nail or pencil, lift the bottom loop up and over the second loop and post, Fig. 2. Continue winding and lifting around the posts in order, weaving the yarn the same way. Each time you weave once around the spool, give a gentle tug on the cord coming out the bottom of the spool. After only a few minutes of weaving, the woven cord will come popping out the bottom of the spool. When the weaving is as long as you like, finish off the end by threading the yarn through each of the post loops around the spool, drawing the yarn tight, and knotting it.

TANGRAM PUZZLE

TANGRAM PUZZLE

The TANGRAM PUZZLE is a clever matching game invented a few thousand years ago by an Oriental man named Tan. For a game to endure that long it must have some very special qualities. The open-endedness of the puzzle invites the player to apply elements of imagination and creative ability, each player at his own level. A very young kid will play with the shapes as building blocks or arrange the puzzle pieces in abstract patterns that help develop his sense of spatial relationships. An older child will find solving the Tangram picture puzzles intellectually stimulating, while helping to develop skills of logic and manipulation. Even an adult will find the seven-piece puzzle challenging—and a kid always feels flattered if a parent enjoys the same game he does.

MATERIALS

heavy cardboard or a square carpet tile, floor
   tile, ceiling tile or any flat material

TOOLS

something to cut the material—scissors,
   knife, etc.
ruler
pencil

CONSTRUCTION

Any flat material of almost any size can be used to make the puzzle pieces. It is easier to start with a perfect square like a carpet tile, but you can make a square from any flat material you can cut. Follow the pattern in Fig. 1 and copy or trace the lines onto your own square.

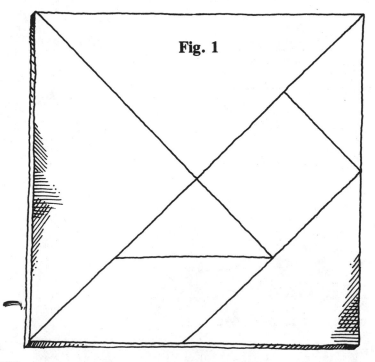

Fig. 1

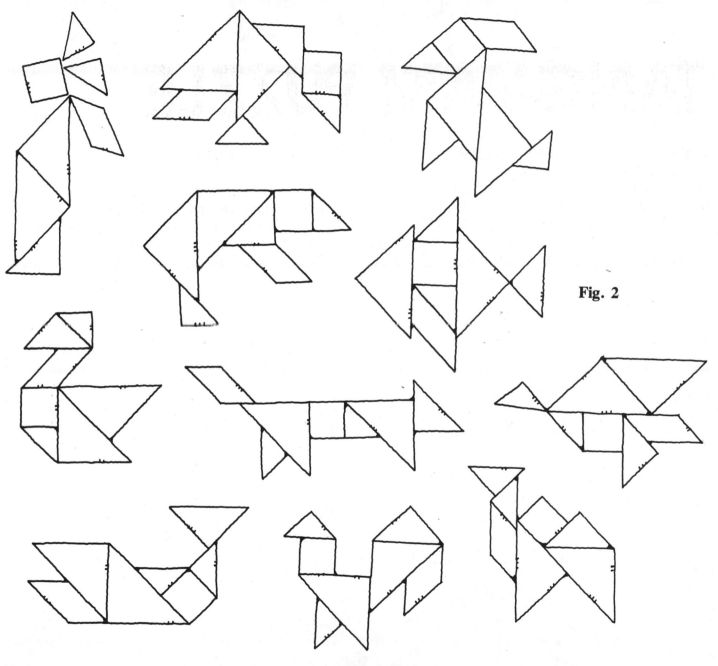

Fig. 2

Use a pencil and ruler and try to keep the exact proportions. If you have had some lessons in geometry, you can lay out the pattern precisely by using a forty-five degree triangle. Cut out the seven pieces of the TANGRAM PUZZLE.

HOW TO PLAY

Fig. 2 shows only a few of the many hundreds of Tangram picture puzzles possible.

Start by trying to arrange the seven puzzle pieces to make one of the pictures, then try another picture. Use the puzzle pieces either side up. However, you must obey two Tangram rules: all seven puzzle pieces must be used for each picture and no two puzzle pieces can overlap. To make the game more difficult, trace only the outline of the pictures in Fig. 2 and see if you—or anyone else—can solve the picture puzzle using the outline only. You might even try to create your own picture puzzles.

TIC-TAC-TROUBLE

TIC-TAC-TROUBLE

Games of skill and strategy, rather than of pure chance, allow a kid to compete—even with adults. It is a player's skill at developing tactics that often give him the advantage to win. The more opportunity to develop strategy, even on a simple game level, the more a kid learns to anticipate and plan ahead. It is also important that all players agree to the same rules, so that everyone has an equal chance to win.

In the simple game of tic-tac-toe, the strategies are few, and once learned by both players, many games end in a draw. TIC-TAC-TROUBLE is a variation that involves the need for ongoing and less repetitive strategies. Rarely does TIC-TAC-TROUBLE end in a draw.

HOW TO PLAY

Draw a regular tic-tac-toe grid on a piece of paper (two lines down and two lines across). Each of the two players uses three game markers. A player's markers should all be the same, but different from his opponent's markers. For game markers you might use coins, buttons, beans, or scraps of paper with your initials.

The two players, in turn, begin to play a regular tic-tac-toe game, placing their markers in the squares, one at a time, in an effort to get three of their own markers in a row (across, up-and-down, or diagonally). If neither player has won after all six markers have been placed

on the grid, the players continue, in turn, to move their own markers, one at a time, to an adjacent unoccupied space on the grid. You can move up-and-down or across only—not diagonally. The first player to get three of his own markers in a row is the winner.

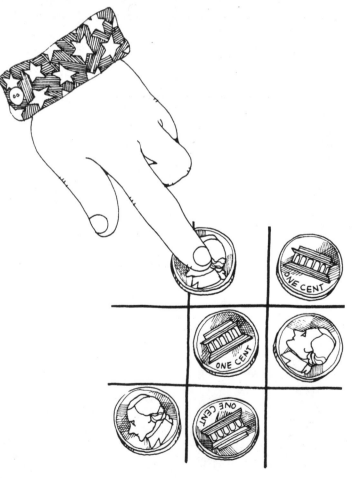

202

NUMBER TIC-TAC-TOE

$3 + 4 + 8 = 15$
I win!

This is yet another version of tic-tac-toe that involves winning strategy and planning—and the ability to add single numbers up to 15.

Numbers and computations seem to give many kids apprehension, but fun and play with numbers can help take away the fear.

NUMBER TIC-TAC-TOE, although simple to play, can be very tricky, and you must plan ahead to win.

HOW TO PLAY

Draw a regular nine space tic-tac-toe grid. One player uses the even numbers 2, 4, 6, 8, and 10, and the other player uses the odd numbers 1, 3, 5, 7, and 9. Both players, in turn, place a number in any space on the grid. Each number can be used only once. The first player to complete a row in any direction that totals 15 (including, possibly, the opponent's numbers) is the winner. At first it might be easier if each player writes his numbers on small scraps of paper to use as markers. Later, when familiar with the game, a player can just write the numbers in the grid as he plays.

Try playing a game of adding up numbers to 13, 16, or any other number up to 20.

SECRET
CODES

SECRET CODES

In any country, most people speak and write the same language, so it is sometimes difficult to send a written message to a pal that no one but you two can understand. If you and a friend share a SECRET CODE, however, no one else will know what your message says—not even parents. When you write a message in code, you are *encoding* it. To read the message, you must *decode* it.

Once you have written your coded message, think of a good way to deliver it. Maybe you and your friend can decide on a special place to leave your secret message for a "pick up." There are many places you might hide the message—under a doormat, in a book, inside bicycle handlebars, under almost anything; or you can fly it like a paper plane, or send it through the mail. Remember, no one will be able to read the message if they don't know the code.

MATERIALS

scrap paper
pencil or pen
lightweight cardboard

ADD-A-LETTER-CODE

Some SECRET CODES can be quite simple, like printing each word backwards.

TNOD DAER SIHT TUO DUOL

But if you want to be certain that not just anyone can figure out your code, try this.

On a piece of paper, write out the secret message you want to send. Using a special "code letter" that only you and your friend know. Add that agreed-upon letter to the end of each word in your message, see illustration.

Now write all the letters of the whole message together as one long word. Divide the long word into groups of three letters, onto a clean piece of paper, and send.

To figure out the message, your friend works the SECRET CODE in reverse. First he writes the letters of the three groups of "words" as one long word. The SECRET CODE letter is then removed and the message read. Sometimes you have to be careful not to remove a code letter when it is part of a word in the message.

To make this code even tougher to figure out, you and your friend could add the "backwards code" to the ADD-A-LETTER CODE or write each of the letter groups in reverse.

EGYPTIAN CODE WRITING

This code is especially difficult for someone to figure out, but it is very simple for you and your friend. Make up two identical code cards as shown in Fig. 1, one for you and one for your friend. In this code, each letter of the alphabet has a symbol which is made up of the line shape—either part of the grid or part of the X—that surrounds the letter on the code card. For the letters J to Z, all symbols include a dot in the middle of the line shape. For example:

Ais ⌐, Eis ☐, Tis ◁, Ois ☐, Wis ∨

If you lose your code card or you think some-one has figured out your SECRET CODE, make another pair of code cards and move the letters around to new positions.

Once you are good at codes, you might try combining ADD-A-LETTER CODE and EGYPTIAN CODE WRITING, or inventing your own codes and combinations.

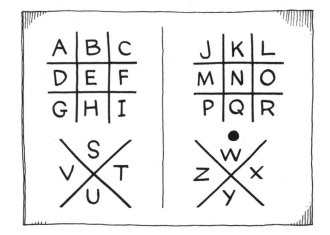

I WILL COME ALONE TONIGHT

DOT AND TRIANGLE —

A pencil and paper game for two or more players

Dot and Triangle is a pencil and paper game for two or more players.

Most kids know how to play the "dot and box" game. In it, a square or rectangular grid made of dots is drawn on paper, and each player in turn connects two adjacent dots. A player tries to make boxes by being the one to add a fourth line to three-line "open boxes" made by previous plays; if he closes the box, he writes his initial in it and gets another turn. At the end of the game, the player who has captured the most boxes is the winner. DOT AND TRIANGLE is a new version of the dot and box game and it is deceptively more difficult.

HOW TO PLAY

Draw a triangular grid of dots with at least eight dots to a side. If there are more than two players, or if you want to play a longer game, add dots to make the triangular grid larger. Each player in turn draws a connecting line between two adjacent dots. Whenever a player on his turn spots any two lines forming two sides of a triangle, he connects the two dots to complete the triangle and writes his initial in-

side. Each time a player captures a triangle he gets another turn which he *must* take even if it means "setting up" the capture of a triangle by his opponent. Most often, the closing of a

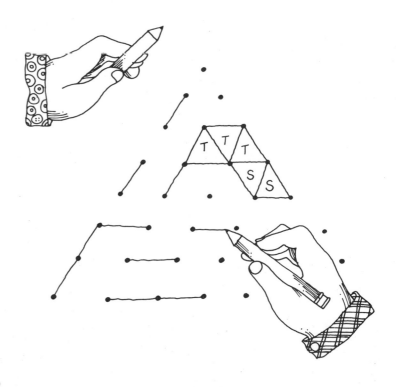

triangle will set up a player's *own* next capture, and since each capture gives him another turn, he can make a "run" of triangles. For the first few turns, each player will be connecting dots that do not set up captures at all. But soon all "safe" lines will have been used, and a player may be forced to give his opponent a capture (he should try not to give him a run, however). In DOT AND TRIANGLE, the "runs" can be very long, sometimes capturing half or more of all the triangles. So learn to think ahead and plan your moves. When all the triangles have been captured, the player with the most is the winner.

DOUBLE NUMBER MAZE

DOUBLE NUMBER MAZE —

A pencil and paper game for two or more players

When a young kid's interest in numbers is developed through play activities, he will usually adapt to school mathematics quite effortlessly. The same theory applies to letters. A young child's ability with the alphabet is usually limited to the letters in his name, but game situations that allow a kid to practice the entire alphabet will encourage later reading and writing skills. The DOUBLE NUMBER MAZE is one of the best games to practice number (and letter) recognition, and is also an exciting game that can be played by the entire family. Because the only materials needed are a pencil and paper, the DOUBLE NUMBER MAZE can be played almost anywhere. On your next family outing to a restaurant, try playing the DOUBLE NUMBER MAZE on the back of a paper placemat while waiting for the food to be served.

PRELIMINARIES

On a notebook-size or larger sheet of paper, write the numbers 1 through 20 so that they are randomly scattered all over. Now write the numbers 1 through 20 again all over the paper trying not to have matching numbers too near each other. To make a "double letter maze," use the letters A through Z so that there are two of each letter randomly scattered on the paper. If a young child helps to do the writing, do not be concerned about number or letter reversals. A child just learning will recognize and correct his own printing mistakes in time. Now the game is ready to play.

HOW TO PLAY

The object of the DOUBLE NUMBER MAZE is to connect the duplicate numbers (or letters) with pencil lines so that no line touches or crosses another line. Each player in turn connects two matching numbers with a line, starting with the two 1's and proceeding in order through 20. You do not have to draw the shortest route between two numbers. You can draw a long, winding line to purposely foul up your opponent. Usually the game begins to get tough when you reach the 14's and 15's. The first player who cannot connect two matching numbers without his line touching or crossing another line is the loser.

SIMPLE MAGIC

SIMPLE MAGIC

At the age when a child begins to concoct strange "potions" in the kitchen and claims magical powers for certain words or possessions, he also develops an enormous appetite for magic tricks. A kid will delight at having simple magic performed, then immediately wish to duplicate the tricks himself. One of the finest thrills for a child is to be let in on the secret and then mystify others with "his" magic. But many tricks depend on special devices or sleights that require patience and dedicated practice to perform. That's fine if a child has the desire to pursue magic as a hobby, but if he hasn't, he can still perform effective feats of magic by just learning a few simple secrets.

Most of the magic tricks that follow require very little manipulation or technique and can be done quite casually by children, even under close scrutiny, without "goofing." It's hard, however, for anyone to learn a new trick and immediately perform it well on family and friends. If a trick fails or gets messed up, a smile and the phrase, "Well, I guess I forgot to say the right magic words," will smooth things over. Then the trick should be tried again.

Even simply done magic can bewilder the spectator, but a trick performed with a little story or side talk and an aura of mystery will entertain and convince an audience much more. A kid might start a magic trick by claiming that he can do something that is seemingly impossible, or he might talk about some special "magical power" he possesses. Each child's unique personality dictates the style of his performance. His ability to present a trick will improve the more he performs it.

Most magicians say that if you reveal the secret you break the spell. Of course, you don't have to tell how you did a trick, but most kids are anxious not only to puzzle their friends, but delight in showing how the miracle was done. Then there's the person who claims to know the "secret" of your magic. Maybe he does, but probably not. The smart performer just smiles and goes on to the next trick. Or he invites the "know-it-all" to try it himself!

ALMOST IMPOSSIBLE CARD GAME

As soon as a kid can count from 1 through 13, he is ready for the challenge of simple card games (and old enough to understand the meaning of rules). Games with cards often help give a kid confidence about his number ability and encourage him to use numbers in everyday situations. The ALMOST IMPOSSIBLE CARD GAME is a solitaire game to play alone or a game of chance for challenging friends, but, as the name implies, it's almost impossible.

All you need is a complete deck of playing cards. You play the game by turning over all fifty-two cards, one at a time, while calling out the regular card sequence: "ace, two, three, four" and so forth through "king." When you reach the end of the sequence you start again, "ace, two, three" and so forth, until you've gone through the deck. The object is to always be *wrong*, that is, to find you've mismatched your call with the turned-over card. If you are wrong for every card in the deck, you win, but if the card you call out matches the card you just turned over, you lose.

Begin by removing the jokers from the deck, and shuffle the cards. Place the deck on a table, face side down. Say "ace" and turn over the first card. If the card *is* an ace then you lose right away, but if not then say "two" and turn over the next card. If it is not a "2", then say "three" and continue to count and turn over the cards one at a time. If you count through "jack, queen, king" and still have not been caught by a matching number and card, then start with "ace" again, and continue counting. If you count "ace" to "king" four times and don't get a match, then you have won. It may sound easy to win, but it is almost impossible. In fact, the odds against your winning are about sixty-four to one. Be sure to shuffle the cards before each new game. If you want to play the ALMOST IMPOSSIBLE CARD GAME with a friend, see who can go through the most cards in the deck before being caught by a match.

PAPER CLIP
AND STRIP TRICK

PAPER CLIP AND STRIP TRICK
(and Tongue Twister)

Before you even try this trick, say the name three times—fast. Paper Clip and Strip Trick, Paper Clip and Strip Trick, Paper Clip and Strip Trick. Say it without reading the words. If you can do that, the rest of the trick is simple.

As with so many tricks, knowing a good magic word can help. You might try the standard "Abracadabra" or "Hocus Pocus" or maybe say "Paper Clip and Strip Trick" three times. Your own made-up magic word will sound more convincing.

CONSTRUCTION AND WORKING

Cut or tear a strip of paper a few inches wide and a foot or so long. The exact size isn't important. (Paper for an adding machine works well.) Curve one end of the paper strip around until it touches the strip just past the middle. Fasten it in place with a paper clip. Now curve the other end around the back side of the strip and fasten it in place with a second paper clip as shown in the illustration. Using both hands

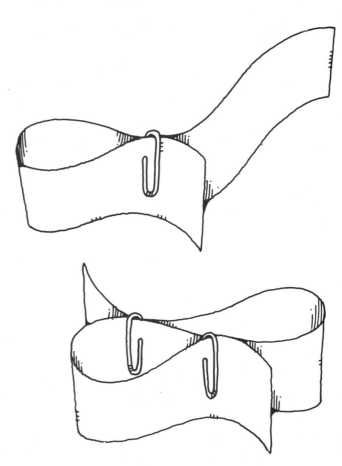

218

hold the two ends of the paper strip firmly. (You might have a subject from the audience hold one of the strip ends for you.) Say the magic words and briskly pull the two strip ends in opposite directions. If the magic works, the paper strip will pull flat and the two paper clips will shoot in the air and hitch themselves together. Let your audience inspect the connected clips and try to figure out how it was done. If you want to figure it out, repeat the trick for yourself but pull the strip ends slowly and watch how the clips attach. Of course, tell your audience that the magic words made the trick work.

The only practice you may need is knowing how hard or fast to pull the paper strip ends: not too fast, not too slow. Practice a few times until you get the "feel." Then you are ready to perform. Should the trick fail—and sometimes even the best magic words don't help—just set it up and try again.

MAGIC NUMBER CARDS

1	21	41	61	81
3	23	43	63	83
5	25	45	65	85
7	27	47	67	87
9	29	49	69	89
11	31	51	71	91
13	33	53	73	93
15	35	55	75	95
17	37	57	77	97
19	39	59	79	99

4	15	30	45	60	71
5	20	31	46	61	76
6	21	36	47	62	77
7	22	37	52	63	78
12	23	38	53	68	79
13	28	39	54	69	84
14	29	44	55	70	85

64	70	76	82	88	94
65	71	77	83	89	95
66	72	78	84	90	96
67	73	79	85	91	97
68	74	80	86	92	98
69	75	81	87	93	99

2	22	42	62	82
3	23	43	63	83
6	26	46	66	86
7	27	47	67	87
10	30	50	70	90
11	31	51	71	91
14	34	54	74	94
15	35	55	75	95
18	38	58	78	98
19	39	59	79	99

8	24	40	56	72	88
9	25	41	57	73	89
10	26	42	58	74	90
11	27	43	59	75	91
12	28	44	60	76	92
13	29	45	61	77	93
14	30	46	62	78	94
15	31	47	63	79	95

16	24	48	56	80	88
17	25	49	57	81	89
18	26	50	58	82	90
19	27	51	59	83	91
20	28	52	60	84	92
21	29	53	61	85	93
22	30	54	62	86	94
23	31	55	63	87	95

32	38	44	50	56	62
33	39	45	51	57	63
34	40	46	52	58	96
35	41	47	53	59	97
36	42	48	54	60	98
37	43	49	55	61	99

Using the seven MAGIC NUMBER CARDS you can tell someone exactly what number he is thinking of. Ask your subject to think of any number between one and one hundred. You might suggest your subject think of his lucky number, age, weight, or height in inches. Then, without revealing the number, have your subject point to the MAGIC NUMBER CARDS which contain that number. You seem to concentrate for a moment and then you tell your subject exactly what number he was thinking of. And you are correct!

THE SECRET

The number in the upper left-hand corner of each MAGIC NUMBER CARD is the key number! To figure out the number someone is thinking of, just add the key numbers on the cards the subject pointed to. With a little practice, you will soon memorize the key number of each card, and be able to add them in your head quickly.

CONSTRUCTION

You will need seven pieces of scrap paper or cardboard, and a pencil or pen. Following the illustration exactly, make each of the seven MAGIC NUMBER CARDS. Be sure to include *all* the numbers shown, but only those numbers for a given card. Keep the numbers in the same order so that the key number is always first.

FOUR MAGIC CARDS

You have four cards, each with a different single number written on each side. Select a subject from the audience. Write a number prediction on a scrap of paper, fold it up, and give it to your subject. Lay out the four cards and ask your subject to turn over only one but any one of the cards, and add up the four numbers showing. The subject tells you the sum of the numbers. Then you ask him to check your prediction of that total—and you are correct!

THE SECRET

Tear four squares of paper from scrap paper, or use four paper cards. With a crayon, pencil or marking pen, write the numbers 1 through 8 on the cards so that each card has an odd number on one side and an even number on the other side in the order shown in the illustration: 1 with 2 on the reverse side; 3 with 4 on the reverse side; 5 with 6 on the reverse side; 7 with 8 on the reverse side. Let your subject inspect the FOUR MAGIC CARDS, then place them down individually so that only the *odd* numbers show (1, 3, 5, and 7).

If you add the four odd numbers, they will always equal 16. Since the value of the number on the back side of any one of the cards is 1 greater than the value on the face side, whatever card your subject turns over will add 1 to the total of 16 and give 17. Therefore, your prediction will always be 17 and you will always be correct. Of course, you can do the same trick and ask your subject to turn over two or three cards. For each card that is turned over, you add 1 to the key number, 16, and you can predict the sum. For example, if you ask that three cards be turned over, your prediction would be 19 (16 plus 3).

AN ESP VARIATION

Use the same FOUR MAGIC CARDS. Select a subject, give him the four cards, and ask that he arrange them in his hand with any four numbers showing. Instruct your subject to hold the cards so that you cannot see them, or you might turn your back or be blindfolded. Ask your subject to add the sum of the four digits showing and then to concentrate on that number. Now use your showmanship and seem to concentrate but tell your subject you are having some difficulty and it would be helpful if he told you how many *odd*-number cards were showing. Your subject responds and you seem to concentrate again. Then you tell him the sum of the cards he is holding and you are correct!

THE SECRET

You subtract the number of odd cards that you are told are showing from 20 and that gives you the correct sum. For example, if your subject tells you that 2 odd cards are showing, then the correct number for the sum of the subject's cards would be 18 (20 less 2). Since you know how the "basic trick" works, see if you can figure out the ESP VARIATION.

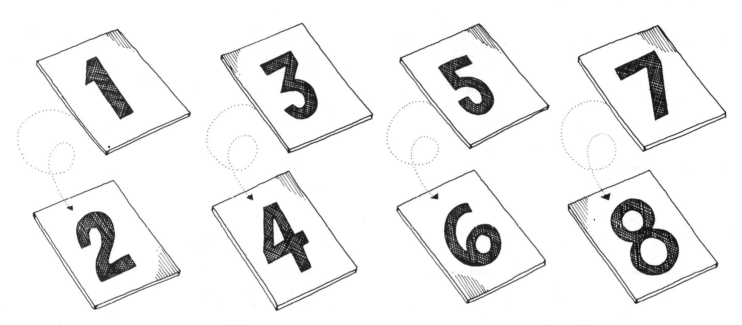

5 CHOICE ESP

Start with a regular deck of cards and deal out five piles, each pile containing a different number of cards. Ask your subject to concentrate on one—and only one—of the card piles. As your subject concentrates, pretend to read his mind, and then write a prediction on a scrap of paper. Fold the paper once or twice to conceal the prediction and put it down. Now ask your subject to reveal which pile he was thinking of. You turn over the cards in that pile and ask your subject to read the prediction. Your prediction says, "You will choose the 5 pile." You are correct—and your subject is amazed.

THE SECRET

Your written prediction is always the

same—"You will choose the five pile"— because each of the piles *is* the "5 pile." Before you start the trick, arrange the deck so that when you deal out the cards, the piles contain cards similar to those shown in the illustration. The first pile can be any number of cards *more* than five; the second pile contains cards with card values that add up to five; the third pile contains the four fives in the deck; the fourth pile contains any five cards; and the last pile is similar to the first and contains any number of cards more than five.

If your subject selects the first pile, count the piles from right to left and it *is* the 5 pile. The second pile is the 5 pile because the values of the cards add up to five. The third pile, of course, contains all four fives in the deck. The fourth pile is the 5 pile because it is the only pile containing exactly five cards. And the fifth pile is the 5 pile counting left to right.

There are two important rules to this trick. First, only turn over the pile that the subject selects, and second, never repeat the trick with the same subject or he will surely catch on.

MELTING HANDKERCHIEFS

This is a close-up magic trick and can be done right under the eyes of your audience; indeed, you should invite your audience to watch really closely. Two ordinary handkerchiefs are shown and inspected, then each of the handkerchiefs is rolled up diagonally. You then wrap the two handkerchiefs around each other several times so that they are definitely twisted together and appear knotted. But when you say the magic words and pull on the ends of the handkerchiefs, the twists and knots seem to melt, and the two handkerchiefs pull apart. Perform the trick as many times as your audience asks.

THE SECRET

You will have to learn how to fold the handkerchiefs in a special way. Use two large cloth handkerchiefs. Cloth napkins or silk scarves will also be fine. Roll each handkerchief diagonally in the shape of a fat rope, Fig. 1. Hold out your left hand, palm up, and put one of the rolled handkerchiefs across your fingertips. Put the other handkerchief perpendicularly across the first, Fig. 2. To make the method clear, the ends of the handkerchiefs have been labeled A, B, C, and D in the illustration. Using both hands, wrap end A under and

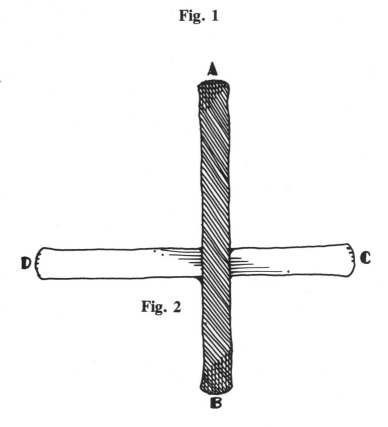

Fig. 1

Fig. 2

around end D, Fig. 3. Now wrap end D under and around end A, Fig. 4. Finally, fold end C under the center to meet end D, and fold end B under the center to meet end A, Fig. 5. The last step must be done in the order given or the trick won't work. Now hold ends A and B in one hand, and ends C and D in the other hand. After saying the magic words, pull the pairs of ends apart. The handkerchiefs will appear to melt through each other. If you want to discover how the illusion works, do the trick for yourself using rope instead of handkerchiefs. As you pull the rope ends, you can see that the ropes were not knotted at all. You will also learn not to do the MELTING HANDKERCHIEF trick with rope or everyone might figure it out!

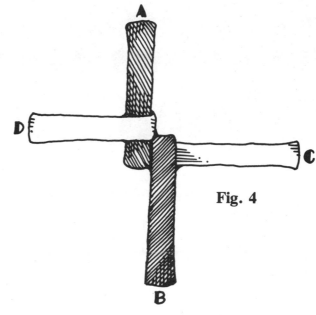

Fig. 4

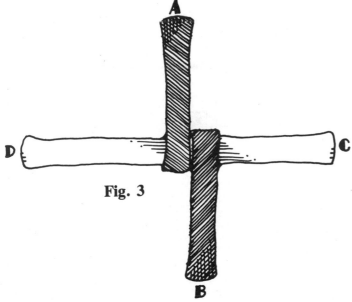

Fig. 3

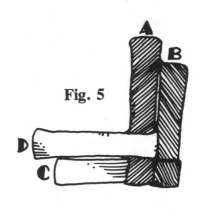

Fig. 5

PREDICTION DOMINO

This trick is best done when you and your friends happen to be playing a regular game of dominoes. Before a new round is started, you claim to have special magical powers and can predict what the two numbers on the end "halves" of the two end dominoes of the chain will be when the game is completed. In fact, you will even write your prediction on a piece of paper to be folded over and put it aside until the end of the game. Begin the domino game as usual with a "double" and match the domino ends to form a "chain." When all the dominoes have been added to the chain, have all the players note the numbers on the two end halves of the domino chain. Then ask one of the players to open your prediction. Of course, you are correct.

THE SECRET

The trick to **PREDICTION DOMINO** is knowing the fact that whenever a game of dominoes uses all the pieces to form a continuous chain, the two "half" end numbers on each of the end dominoes will always match. Therefore, any domino removed from the chain will

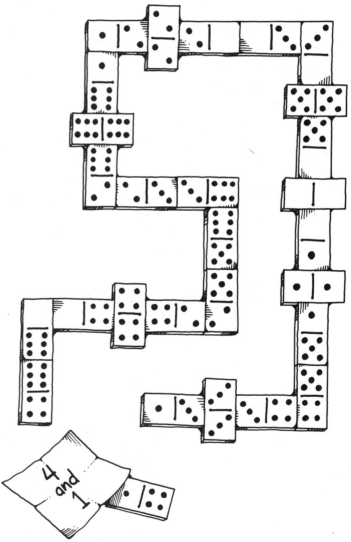

228

match the end of the broken chain. However, for the trick to work, you must start with a complete set of twenty-eight pieces. Before the game begins, you secretly remove one domino piece (but not a "double") from the whole collection, and note the number of dots on each

end. Those two numbers will be the prediction that you write. Keep the domino piece hidden until the end of the game. If the other players ask, you can repeat the trick, but secretly replace the first domino and remove a new one.

CALENDAR MAGIC

There are many simple mathematical relationships between the numbers on a calendar that are not obvious to an audience when you present them as magic. The three CALENDAR MAGIC tricks that follow are simple to understand and perform, yet will boggle some kids and most grown-ups. The only materials necessary to do CALENDAR MAGIC are a calendar from any year, a pencil or pen, and some note paper for calculations.

ROW OF 3

Select a subject and hand him a calendar. Without letting you see, have your subject

choose any month and circle any three consecutive dates in a horizontal row on that calendar page. Ask your subject to add the three dates and tell you only the total. Almost immediately you name the three dates circled—and you are correct!

THE SECRET

There is a simple formula that will allow you to calculate the three dates from just the total your subject announces. First, divide the total by 3 and the number you get will be the middle date. Then subtract 1 from the middle date to get the first date and add 1 to the middle date to get the third date. For example, if your subject tells you that 60 is the total of three consecutive dates in a calendar row, divide 60 by 3 to get the 20th as the middle date. Subtract 1 and the 19th is the first date, add 1 and the 21st is the third date. ROW OF 3 might seem baffling to your audience, but it is really simple.

COLUMN OF 3

This CALENDAR MAGIC is a variation of ROW OF 3. Have your subject choose any month of the calendar and circle any three consecutive dates in a column so that you cannot see his choice. Ask your subject for the total of those three dates circled—and within seconds you reveal the chosen dates.

THE SECRET

Divide the total by 3 to get the middle date; subtract 7 to calculate the top date; add 7 to get the bottom date.

BLOCK OF 9

For this CALENDAR MAGIC trick, you and your subject might have to do some figuring with pencil and paper. Select a subject and hand him a calendar, pencil, and note paper. Have your subject choose any calendar month and draw a square block around any nine dates (three equal rows across and three equal rows down, see illustration) so that you cannot see his choice. Now ask your subject to tell you only the smallest number date in the block. Do some quick figuring, then tell your subject and the audience the total sum of all nine dates—

and as usual, you are correct. Let your subject add the dates and check for himself.

THE SECRET

The formula trick for BLOCK OF 9 is quite simple but it usually requires pencil and paper calculations. Add 8 to the smallest number your subject states, and multiply the total by 9. The result will be the sum of all nine dates in the BLOCK OF 9. For example, if your subject states 7 as the smallest number, add 8 and 7 for a total of 15, and multiply 15 by 9 to get 135 as the sum. As your math skills develop, you may not have to do any pencil figuring at all.

MYSTERIOUS SILVER BALL

MYSTERIOUS SILVER BALL

Show your audience a silver ball made of crumpled aluminum foil with a string through its middle. Hold the string vertically, one hand at the top end, the other at the bottom. The ball, will of course, drop down the string. Swing your hands around to reverse top and bottom positions, and let the ball drop down the string again. Do this a few more times and then tell the audience that the MYSTERIOUS SILVER BALL while dropping will stop anywhere along the string at the command of "Stop" and continue to drop at the command "Go." Select a subject from the audience and have him call out the commands. The MYSTERIOUS SILVER BALL will be very obedient and the audience amazed.

THE SECRET

The hole through the aluminum ball is not put in straight up-and-down but offset, that is, the hole goes in one side of the ball and comes out the other end *at an angle*. With the offset hole, the ball will drop down the string if the ends are held a bit loose. If the string is pulled taut the offset hole will act as a brake and stop the ball. Release the tension on the string and the ball will drop again. Once you have practiced, you will get the feel of just how hard to pull both ends of the string to make the MYSTERIOUS SILVER BALL stop, and how relaxing the tension slightly will allow the ball to drop without the audience ever suspecting how it is all done.

MATERIALS

aluminum foil
heavy string

TOOLS

fat nail or pointed pencil

CONSTRUCTION

Tear off a length of aluminum foil—about a foot or two long—and crumple it up tightly in

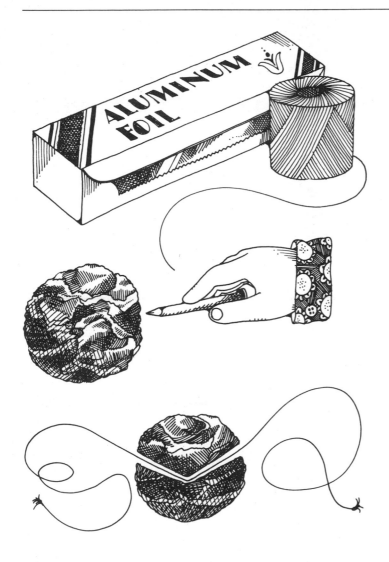

hole at an angle so that it meets the first hole in the center of the ball. Hold the ball up and look through one end of the hole. Although the hole goes all the way through, you should *not* be able to see through. If you can, the trick will not work, so make another ball and be sure that the two hole openings are not directly opposite, but at angles to each other. Cut a length of heavy string about three or four feet long and thread one end through the hole in the ball and out the other. The trick is now ready to perform.

your hands to make a ball. Follow the illustration carefully. Poke a hole in one side of the ball with a large nail or pointed pencil, but go into the ball only half way. Now poke another hole in the ball from the other side but *not* directly beneath the first hole. Aim the second

PENDULUM PREDICTIONS

Some magic tricks are truly mysterious and cannot be explained by logic. The PENDULUM will answer any questions you ask with a definite yes or no. Will you receive a letter tomorrow? Is it going to rain on Saturday? Maybe it is just luck, but the PENDULUM PREDICTIONS will almost always be correct. Why? No one seems to know.

To have the PENDULUM answer your questions, place your elbow on a table top with your arm up, and hold the pendulum string between your fingers. You can hold the pendulum in one hand and put your other hand under the ring to ask the questions yourself. Or have another person ask the questions, and ask him to place his hand flat on the table under the pendulum ring. Shorten or lengthen the string so that the ring is above and not touching the hand. Ask the question, and watch for the pendulum's answer.

You may have to wait a minute for the pendulum to move. If the pendulum swings in a circle the answer is *yes*, if the pendulum swings in a straight line, the answer is *no*. The magic

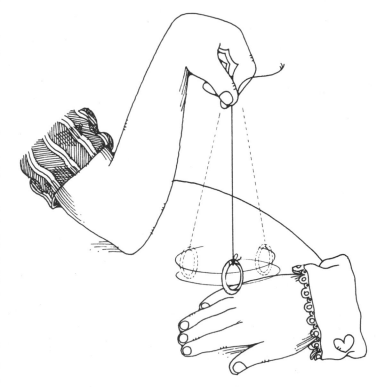

works for anyone: it is the pendulum that has the magic, not the person holding the string or asking the questions. On rare occasions the pendulum will not move at all. If that happens, assume the pendulum does not know the answer and begin again with a new question. Do you have an idea how the mysterious pendulum works? Is it the power of suggestion? Are the magical powers present in the room? Maybe in the ring? If you have any idea, ask the pendulum if it is right, yes, or not, no.

MATERIALS

any kind of ring (finger ring, large washer or nut, piece of hollow bone, drapery ring, etc.)
string

TOOLS

scissors

CONSTRUCTION

Tie a piece of string to the ring and you are ready for PENDULUM PREDICTIONS.

PLAIN PAPER CUP

PLAIN PAPER CUP

Did you ever need something just at a time when you didn't have it? It happens to everyone once in a while, and you have to "make do" with what you do have. Carrying water was an important job before there were pipes to bring the water to you. People usually carried water in wooden buckets, but sometimes a bucket would break or maybe dry out and leak, so people had to "make do" with whatever else was at hand to carry the water. A temporary water carrier could be made quickly by folding a square piece of canvas into a watertight cloth bucket. The same pattern for folding a cloth bucket can be used to make a drinking cup from a plain sheet of paper. A PLAIN PAPER CUP is a "make do" project that will come in handy any time you need a water cup, but don't have one. Then you too will know how to "make do."

CONSTRUCTION

The only material you need is a plain piece of notebook paper cut into the largest square possible (Fig. 1). Bring two corners of the paper together, and crease it flat on the diagonal to form a double-thickness triangle, Fig. 2. Fold a base corner of the triangle over so that it just touches the middle of the side opposite it and crease, Fig. 3. Repeat the procedure with the other base corner, Fig. 4. There will be two

small triangular "ears" pointing up from the top of the folded paper. Fold one ear over the front and crease, then fold the other ear over the back and crease, Fig. 5. Pop open the PLAIN PAPER CUP, fill it with water, and have a drink.

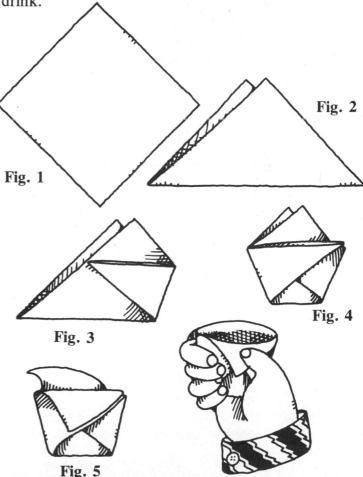

Fig. 1

Fig. 2

Fig. 3

Fig. 4

Fig. 5

SUGGESTED MINIMUM AGES

These are *suggested* minimum ages only; as a parent, you will know your child's interests and abilities best. Ages listed between columns indicate projects in which playing and making are the same activity.

QUICKIES

If you ever need an activity for the kids really fast and you don't have the time to prepare or help out, try some of these PLAYBOOK projects.

BEST FRIENDS

If you and a best friend are looking for something to do, these are some of the PLAYBOOK projects you can share.

SECRET LIST (for kids only)

Have you done something your parents don't like and been sent to your room? Well, your room isn't such a bad place to play. And if you have a normally stocked kid's room with most of the materials and tools to do some of these projects, your punishment won't seem quite so boring.